D0825364

AN ANTHOLOGY OF ELIZABETHAN LUTE SONGS, MADRIGALS, AND ROUNDS

MUSIC EDITED BY
NOAH GREENBERG

TEXT EDITED BY
W. H. AUDEN
AND
CHESTER KALLMAN

The Norton Library
W · W · NORTON & COMPANY · INC ·
NEW YORK

ISBN 0 393 00520 8

PRINTED IN THE UNITED STATES OF AMERICA

7 8 9 0

CONTENTS

Contents

Contents

Contents

Contents

Contents

MADRIGALS AND ROUNDS

DAVID MELVILL
dates unknown

THOMAS MORLEY
1558–1603

JOHN WILBYE
1574–1638

INDEX OF FIRST LINES 239

INDEX OF POETS 242

INTRODUCTION

THE POEMS

All the songs in this collection were written in a space of only twenty-five years, and the whole period of the English madrigalists and lutanists is no more than forty. What makes this brief moment one of the most extraordinary events in cultural history is the miraculous coincidence of composers and lyric poets of equal high quality. Moreover, the former did not have to depend on one or two poets; more than half the lyrics they set come down to us unsigned, yet even these, in all their stylistic variety, are no whit inferior to those written by the identifiable or the famous.

There is no better period, therefore, to study if one is interested in the relation between poetry and music, and in the influence, if any, which they exert on each other. There are two schools of thought which either deny or deplore their relation. The first is made up of persons who love poetry but have no feeling for the human singing voice, though they may claim to admire instrumental music. They base their objection to vocal music upon observations which are, in themselves, correct: that, whenever verse is set to notes, its rhythm is distorted and that, however precise a singer's diction, a listener who is not already familiar with the words will at best catch half of them.

The second, made up of singing fans, observing, again correctly, that very beautiful arias have been written to trivial or downright silly verses, conclude that all a composer requires from a poet are so and so many syllables of such and such a quality, and that their meaning is irrelevant. They quote Rossini's remark, "Give me a laundry-list and I will set it," unaware, apparently, that a laundry-list, or any list for that matter, has a poetic value, and one which is exceptionally translatable into musical terms. It might be difficult, however, to resist their arguments were there, in the period we are covering, many examples like Byrd's "Although the heathen poets," where an unresolved subordinate clause has been set quite happily. Mercifully, it is very much an exception.

Then, to confuse matters, there are the crank prosodists who attempt to scan verse by musical notation, provoking the orthodox, like Sir George Saintsbury, to conclude that the less a poet knows about music, the better; indeed it is probably best for him to be, like Shelley, tone-deaf.

Yet the output of vocal music between 1588 and 1632 remains. Here are scores of poems, the poetic quality of which satisfies the most exacting of the song-hating school, which were written directly for the purpose of being set, and would not have come into being had the composers not existed to set them; here are scores of part-songs and solos, the musical value of which satisfies the most exacting of the syllable-for-voice school, the stimulus to which was, nevertheless, a good poem.

It is always possible, of course, to assert—because the assertion cannot be proved or disproved—that the poets would have written better if they had written only for the speaking voice, and that the composers would have done as well or better with bad verses, but one thing is certain: both the poems and the music would have been different.

The questions which will naturally arise in the literary reader's mind are two: From an examination of these poems, is it possible to learn what characteristics a good poem must possess in order to be settable? and: Are some of the characteristics of these poems, which, read apart from the music, make them good, the result of their having been written to be set?

Any consideration of such questions must begin with the difference between musical rhythm, in any style of music, and verse rhythm, in any language. In music a difference in temporal duration between two notes is more noticeable than a difference in accentuation; musical "prosody," so to speak, is always quantitative, not qualitative, and in a much stricter way than any spoken verse can be which, like Greek or classical Latin, is scanned quantitatively. If in quantitative scansion syllables are classified as either long or short, every long syllable being temporally equivalent to two short syllables, this classification, when applied to a spoken language, is, strictly speaking, a fiction, for probably no two spoken syllables are of exactly the same length. But in music, for any given metronome marking, all quarter notes, say, are identical in duration. Also, instead of there being only two kinds of lengths, there are infinite possibilities of sustaining or subdividing notes. When, therefore, a line of verse in any language, no matter what its prosodic principle, is sung, the rhythm the ear perceives is based on differences in length. Differences in accent are also often perceptible, but they are always secondary. Further, the ear's judgment of tempo when hearing music is quite different when hearing speech: a tempo of spoken syllables which feels like an adagio would, if the syllables were musical notes, feel like an allegretto.

By the end of the sixteenth century the English language and the prosodic principles governing its verse had become, in all essentials, what they are today. It had already been established that the normal scansion of English verse should be by feet, not by accent only, like Anglo-Saxon verse, nor by the number of syllables only, like French, but that these feet should consist of various combinations of accented and unaccented syllables, not of the "long" and "short" syllables of classical poetry. Further, it had become clear that the language was favorable to certain kinds of feet and hostile to others. Even at the height of his folly about classical meters in English, Campian noted:

The heroical verse that is distinguisht by the *Dactile* hath bene oftentimes attempted in our English toong, but with passing pitiful successe; and no wonder, seeing it is an attempt altogether against the nature of our language. For both the concourse of our monasillables make our verse unapt to slide, and also if we examine our polysillables, we find few of them by reason of their heaviness, willing to serve in place of a Dactile . . . . . our English monasillables enforce many breathings which no doubt greatly lengthen a verse, so that it is no wonder if for these reasons our English verses of five feete hold pace with the Latines of sixe.

OBSERVATIONS IN THE ART OF ENGLISH POESIE 1602

When poets discover that their language is most easily organized rhythmically by using certain kinds of feet and certain kinds of meters, they tend to fall into the habit of using these exclusively, as if no other kinds were possible. To this habit, a familiarity with the art of vocal music can be a valuable corrective. For, while listening to a song, the verses of which were written, say, in iambics, one hears not only iambics, but any number of other feet, amphibrachs, cretics, tribrachs, spondees, etc., which can suggest to the poet all kinds of rhythmical possibilities for spoken verse. This is particularly true, perhaps, in the case of English, owing to its large number of monosyllabic words, the metrical value of which is not innate but depends on their position in the line. In a language like German, for example, which has an accentual prosody and many polysyllabic words, metrical innovations are much more difficult, for one polysyllabic word in a line can dictate the meter of the rest of the words in it.

If the lyrics of the Elizabethan poets are rhythmically more interesting than those of other periods, it is difficult to escape the conclusion that the close association of poets with musicians of high caliber was largely responsible.

Dryden and Burns are excellent song writers, but their songs have a metrical conventionality from which the Elizabethans were free; and it is to be noticed that those Romantic lyrics which are most exciting rhythmically, like some of Blake's and Beddoes', are consciously modeled on the Elizabethans. The normal conventions of spoken English verse make small provision for monosyllabic feet or for the spondee, and frown on changes of metrical base within a stanza. In these songs we find such things constantly, and very effective they sound when only spoken, e.g.:

Deare, sweet, faire, wise, change, shrinke nor be not weake

Not a friend, not a friend greet
My poor corpse, where my bones shall be throwne.
   A thousand thousand sighes to save, lay me o where
   Sad true lover never find my grave, to weepe there.

   But if you let your lovers mone,
     The Fairie Queene Proserpina,
   Will send abroad her Fairies ev'ry one,
     That shall pinch blacke and blew,
   Your white hands, and faire armes,
     That did not kindly rue
       Your Paramours harmes.

Such lines have indeed, as Saintsbury declares, their own vocal music, but their authors would not have found it, had they not been writing songs.

This seems the right point at which to digress and put in a good word for the "classical" metrical experiments of the Cambridge School, to which Campian belonged. Their attempt, out of a Renaissance idolization of the Ancients, to write in the meters of Greek and Latin poetry, whether quantitatively in exact imitation or in some accentual substitute, was defeated by the nature of the English language. And their rejection of rhyme, from the same motive, though possible, turned out to be an unnecessary deprivation. But English poetry owes much to their forlorn attempt. In art, as in science and almost every human activity, men should never be discouraged from going up blind alleys. They will not find what they are looking for, but they may discover something which a more orthodox investigator would never have come upon. But for this particular blind alley, we should lack certain beautiful poems—for example, that charming lyric of Campian's, *Rose-cheeked Laura, come,* and the magnificent choruses in *Samson Agonistes.* What is more important, it might have taken English poetry a much longer time to escape from the metrical anarchy of the fifteenth and early sixteenth centuries. As that most implacable foe of all "classicizing" has chivalrously admitted:

It is at least possible that Spenser might not have been what he most assuredly is, the founder of modern English prosody and modern English poetic diction alike, had he not gone through this 'distemper' . . . If there is one thing that a study of the classics indicated more than another, it was the necessity of a certain 'standardisation'—the law that verse *has* laws, and cannot be made by merely pitchforking together unselected words, and leaving the heaps to correspond at the hazard of the pitchfork . . . The less definitely the example was taken, the more entirely literal acceptance of the precepts was avoided, the better; but example, and even precept to some extent, could not but establish an atmosphere—set up a tendency and a habit—in the sphere of poetic working.

Saintsbury, HISTORY OF ENGLISH PROSODY

Returning to the influence of music upon verse: this influence affects not only the rhythms of the latter but also its style and content.

Though words take time to say, as notes take time to play, words do not, as notes do, express themselves merely as sounds in temporal motion; they express their meanings as well. In music, that is, the movement is the expression; in poetry it is but a very small part of it. The elements of the poetic vocabulary, therefore, which are best adapted for musical setting are those which require the least reflection to comprehend—its most dynamic and its most immediate. For example: interjections, which in one's mother tongue always sound onomatopoeic (fie, O, alas, adieu); imperatives; verbs of physical motion (going, coming, hasting, following, falling) or physical concomitants of emotions (laughing, weeping, frowning, sighing); adjectives denoting elementary qualities (bright, hard, green, sad); nouns denoting states of feeling (joy, love, rage, despair) or objects, the emotional associations of which are common to all, and strong (sea, night, moon, spring). On the other hand, complicated metaphors which, even if the words are heard, take time to understand and didactic messages which demand assent or dissent are unsuitable. Again, since music, generally speaking, can express only one thing at a time, it is ill adapted to verses which express mixed or ambiguous feelings, and prefers poems which either express one emotional state or successively contrast two states.* Lastly, since words take much longer to sing than to speak, even without the repetitions that music so often requires, poems intended for songs must be short. Ballads and epic chants, in which the music is a subordinate carrier for the words, are another matter.

The poet who would write songs is denied many poetic virtues, but he is also guarded from many poetic vices; he cannot be prolix or private or preachy or obscure. When one compares the poetry of the preceding age, so crowded with endless maundering allegories, with the poems in these song books, one cannot but thank God for men like Byrd and Dowland, in reponse to whose demands the poets were compelled to practice the virtues of graceful ease and conciseness. In illustration of this, let us quote some of the madrigal verses, since these are not represented in this collection.

> *Thus Bonny-boots the birthday celebrated*
> *Of her his lady dearest,*
> *Fair Oriana, which to his heart was nearest.*
> *The nymphs and shepherds feasted*

* It is difficult to imagine an adequate musical setting of Shakespeare's "Farewell, thou art too dear for my possessing," for example. The ambiguous feeling, developed throughout, hinges on the word "dear," with its two meanings of "high in merit" and "expensive;" and one could not expect music to express the simultaneous abnegation and sour mockery of the text.

With clouted cream were, and to sing requested.
 Lo here the fair created,
 Quoth he, the world's chief goddess.
Sing then, for she is Bonny-boot's sweet mistress,
  Then sang the shepherds and nymphs of Diana:
  Long live fair Oriana.

 Weep, O mine eyes, and cease not;
Your spring-tides, out alas, methinks increase not.
 O when, O when begin you
To swell so high that I may drown me in you?

Tan ta ra: cries Mars on bloody rapier.
Fa la la: cries Venus in a chamber.
  Toodle loodle loo:
  Cries Pan, that cuckoo,
  With bells at his shoe,
  And a fiddle too.
But I, alas, lie weeping,
For Death has slain my sweeting,
Which hath my heart in keeping.

Minor poetry, if you like: but how perfect of its kind, how novel and how irreplaceable.

THE TEXT

No one today can concern himself with the Elizabethan song writers without being aware that he is working in the shadow of that great scholar, Dr. Fellowes, and should he feel obliged, as we have felt, to differ from him on some points, it must be with humility and the knowledge that the differences are of minor importance.

In his now classic collection, *English Madrigal Verse*, Dr. Fellowes modernized the spelling and punctuation of the poems. There is much to be said in favor of this course. His book, like ours, was intended not only for scholars, but also, and primarily, for the general reader.

The language of the Elizabethan poets is, in all essential respects, that of our own day. Whereas you cannot modernize a line of, say, Chaucer without destroying both the sound and the rhythm, in the case of these songs it makes almost no difference to what a reader will recite or a singer sing if you print a modernized text or the original. One cannot say that there is a consistent principle which governs the highly erratic spelling of the period when the same word can appear in a poem several times with a different spelling each time. Occasionally, though, modernization can lessen the effect. For example:

> *Noe noe it is the rule to learne a man to woe.*
> *I pray quoth he, nay nay quoth shee,*
> *I pray you let me goe.*

Modernize *woe* to *woo,* and you spoil a rhyme and lose a pun.

The unconventional, by modern standards, punctuation has, at least in the case of the songs, a definite purpose as phrasing direction to the singer, and as a pointer to oratorical pauses it is not simply arbitrary even for spoken verse.

Our decision to print, as far as possible, the original texts has been based on two judgments, a negative and a positive: we believe that the average reader will have no difficulty in following them and that he will find it fun to see what the Elizabethans actually wrote.

However, bearing in mind that this collection is intended for the general public, we have followed modern orthographical practice in the writing of *s* and *v,* and where the original punctuation or spelling (e.g., *then* for *than*) seemed likely to cause a confusion of sense, we have changed it.

In his layout of the stanzas Dr. Fellowes followed nineteenth-century convention; every rhyme word marks the end of a line and indentation is strictly according to line length. Further—though it must be remembered that he was printing the poems without the music—all refrains are reduced to their essential elements.

We have printed the stanzas in the shape in which they appear under the music, not out of mere archaeological piety, but because it seems to us aesthetically better. For instance, where Dr. Fellowes prints

> *Thus, dear damsels, I do give*
> > *Good night, and so am gone.*
> *With your hearts' desires long live,*
> > *Still joy and never moan.*
> > > *Lullaby, lullaby*
> > > > *Hath pleased you*
> > > > *And eased you,*
> > > > > *And sweet slumber seized you*
> > > > > *And now to bed I hie!*

the song book has

> *Thus deare damzells I do give*
> *Good night and so am gone:*
> *With your hartes desires long live,*
> *Still joy, and never mone.*
> *Lulla lullaby, Lulla lullaby*
> *Hath pleasd you and easd you, & sweet slumber sezd you,*
> *And now to bed I hie.*

The difference is not, of course, very important, but it is real.

Three of the lyrics in this collection raise textual problems which merit a special note.

I. MORLEY-BRETON *Faire in a morne,*

The text in *The First Book of Ayres* (1600) runs thus:

Faire in a morne oh fairest morne was ever morne so faire,
When as the sun but not the same that shined in the air,
And on a hill, oh fairest hill was never hill so blessed,
There stood a man was never man for no man so distressed.

But of the earth no earthly Sunne, and yet no earthly creature,
There stoode a face was never face, that carried such a feature.
This man had hap O happie man, no man so hapt as he,
For none had hap to see the hap, that he had hapt to see.

And as he, behold, this man beheld, he saw so faire a face,
The which would daunt the fairest here, and staine the bravest
  grace,
Pittie, he cried, and pittie came, and pittied for his paine,
That dying would not let him die, but gave him life againe.

For joy whereof he made such mirth, that all the world did
  ring,
And Pan *for all his* Nimphs *came forth, to hear the shepherds*
  sing,
But such a song song never was, nor nere will be againe,
Of Philida *the shepheards Queen, and* Coridon *the swaine.*

In the miscellany *England's Helicon* (1600), under the title
Astrophell his song of Phillida and Coridon, appears the following poem by Nicholas Breton.

Faire in a morne, (o fairest morne) was never morne so faire:
There shone a Sunne, though not the Sunne, that shineth in
  the ayre.
For the earth, and from the earth, (was never such a creature:)
Did come this face, (was never face,) that carried such a
  feature.
Upon a hill, (o blessed hill, was never hill so blessed)
There stoode a man, (was never man for woman so distressed.)
This man beheld a heavenly view, which did such vertue give:
As cleares the blind, and helps the lame, and makes the dead
  man live.
This man had hap, (o happy man more happy none then hee;)
For he had hap to see the hap, that none had hap to see.
This silly Swaine, (and silly Swaines are men of meanest
  grace:)
Had yet the grace, (o gracious guest) to hap on such a face.
He pitty cried, and pitty came, and pittied so his paine:
As dying, would not let him die, but gave him life againe.
For joy whereof he made such mirth, as all the woods did ring:

And Pan *with all his Swaines came foorth, to heare the*
   Sheepheard sing.
But such a Song sung never was, nor shall be sung againe:
Of Phillida *the Sheepheards Queene, and* Coridon *the*
   Swaine . . .

One can only describe the relation between these two ver-
sions by saying that Morley's song must be derived from
Breton's poem. It is as if someone, Morley or a friend, with
a good sense of poetry but poor verbal recall, had attempted
to reproduce from memory a poem read and admired some
time back. Even at that, one cannot be altogether certain that
some of the changes—*no man* instead of *woman,* for example
—were not made deliberately. If, as is also quite possible, a
copyist then made errors of his own in transcribing this recalled
version, it is beyond the powers of any human editor to pick
them out from the other differences. By what principle, for
example, did Dr. Fellowes decide to restore *Sunne* in place
of *same* in line 2, but to retain *world* instead of *woods* in
line 13? We have felt justified in making only two emendations,
and these without any certainty that a singer in Morley's time
would have made either. Believing that, even in a song, sense
is preferable to nonsense, we have, as Dr. Fellowes did, in-
terchanged lines 3 and 4 with lines 5 and 6; and, on musical
grounds—the original is possible to sing, but awkward—we have
deleted the *And* from the beginning of line 9.

II. ROSSETER-CAMPIAN *When Laura Smiles,*

In *A Booke of Ayres* (160!), stanza 2, line 1, runs:

   The sprites that remaine in fleeting aire

but from the other stanzas it is clear that the line should be
an iambic alexandrine. Having noticed, one imagines, that in
stanza 4, line 4, occurs the phrase *heav'nly* **spirits,** Dr. Fellowes
takes *sprites* to be a copyist's error and prints the line thus:

   The spirits that remain in fleeting air

which restores an iambic rhythm, but still lacks a foot. In a note, he suggests that the line may have run

> *The wanton spirits that remain in fleeting air.*

This emendation is open to two objections. The adjective *wanton* has already been employed in stanza 1, line 2, and Campian was too careful an artist to make it likely that he would use the same adjective again so soon. Secondly, and more seriously, Rosseter's music demands that the line split up into three phrases of four syllables each, a requirement which Dr. Fellowes' line fails to meet. We make no claims for our own restoration

> *The daintie sprites that still remaine in fleeting aire*

beyond the fact that it changes no words and fits the notes.

III. MELVILL-ANON *O Lusty May*

The only known manuscript of David Melvill's *Booke of Roundels* (1612) is in Australia, and we have been unable to secure a microfilm. All we have had to work with is a modernized transcription.

In the case of this particular song, there are some lines which in their modernized form will not do. For instance, the rhyme scheme of the stanzas is *aabab,* but the transcription of the first two lines of stanza 3 runs

> *Birds on boughs of every sort*
> *Send forth their notes and make great mirth.*

The O.E.D. gives *sorth* as a variant for *sort,* but only for the fifteenth century. Lacking a better idea, we have decided to risk it.

Metrically, the lines are iambic tetrameters, but stanza 5 is transcribed

> *Of all the months of the year,*
> *To mirthful May there is no peer,*

> *Then glistering garments that are so gay,*
> *Ye lovers all make merry cheer*
> *Through gladness of this lusty May.*

Since even the transcribers have archaistically given the noun
balme two syllables under the music, we have ventured to do
the same with months, thus filling out the line. The third line
of the stanza, as transcribed, neither keeps the meter nor
makes sense. On our own responsibility, therefore, we have
emended it to

> *Then glist'ring garments are so gay.*

W. H. Auden
Chester Kallman

INTRODUCTION

THE MUSIC

". . . supper being ended, and the Musicke bookes, according to the custome being brought to the table: the mistresse of the house presented mee with a part, earnestly requesting mee to sing. But when, after many excuses, I protested unfainedly that I could not: everie one began to wonder. Yea, some whispered to others, demanding how I was brought up."

This is a description by the Elizabethan composer and theorist Thomas Morley (*Plaine and Easie Introduction to Practicall Musicke*, 1597) of how a young man came to study music.

Musical life in England reached its highest peak during Elizabethan times. A truly remarkable number of excellent composers wrote music of every description for dancing, singing, the theater, court entertainments, the home and the church, and they wrote for every kind of musical ensemble. Some of it was intended for the skilled performer, some for the amateur; elaborate religious music was written for church services and sacred madrigals for home singing. The greatest master of the period was William Byrd, and some of the others, like Thomas Morley, Orlando Gibbons, Thomas Tomkins, John Wilbye, John Dowland, Anthony Holborne, Thomas Weelkes, while not his equal, were certainly first-rate. But just as the nineteenth century mistakenly regarded the great Handel as England's first important composer, it would be wrong to regard this unusually musical period as "Virgin-born." Elizabeth was an amateur musician because her very musical father Henry saw to it that she received a musical education. Erasmus comments on Henry VIII's great musical abilities, and we know that he surrounded himself with the finest English, Flemish, and Italian composer-performers. He maintained a large collection of instruments in all his establishments, and many early sixteenth-century compositions are attributed to him. The English composers of Henry's day, men like John Taverner and Thomas Tallis, were a continuation of the English school of medieval composers and ranked with the European masters. It should be pointed out that the various national schools of music during the Middle Ages and the Renaissance influenced each other very strongly. John Dunstable, the leading English composer of the 1400s, introduced his style to the Burgundian Court, where it was taken up by its composers and developed into the Burgundian Style. Tallis and Taverner, while continuing the English tradition, reflected continental influence in their large liturgical works. William Byrd was a pupil of Tallis, and many of the Elizabethans were pupils and disciples of Byrd and their church works continued the English tradition.

One of the elements that distinguishes the Elizabethan period from previous periods is the quantity of secular vocal music written then. This we can partly attribute to the Reformation and in larger measure to the Italian vogue then current in England. Italian music was very popular during the entire latter half of the century, and the first important London publication of secular music was a set of Italian madrigals with text translated into English (*Musica Transalpina,* 1588). Even before this, Italian music was imported into England and performed by musicians and amateurs. The English madrigalian publications that followed *Musica Transalpina* used Italian forms, occasionally Italian texts, frequently Italian verse "Englished," set to original music but almost always consciously imitating the Italian masters of the late sixteenth century.

The English Ayre, which forms the main body of this collection, is most often a strophic song for solo voice and accompanying chordal instrument, or, less frequently, a song composed in free form with the entire text set. Often it includes parts for other voices or instruments, but the melody is always in the highest part. This form had its origin on the continent earlier in the century, but it became most popular in Elizabethan England. The Ayre was usually performed by a solo voice with lute. Many of the Elizabethan composers were singer-lutanists and performed their own songs. Some of them, notably John Dowland, traveled widely and their music and performance were known throughout Europe.

From what we know of musical performance then, there was no one manner of presenting a composition. Works written for instrumental ensemble rarely specified which instrument should play a given part. The title page of a Madrigal book would sometimes call for a performance by "Voyces and Violls." Robert Jones says his book of Ayres, *A Musicall Dreame,* ". . . is for one Voyce alone, or to the Lute, the Basse Viole, or both if you please . . ." In the original editions a great number of the songs include not only parts for solo voice, lute, and bass viol, but music for two, three, and four additional musicians. These are so arranged that the performers can place the opened book in the center of a table and read their respective parts from wherever they are seated around it.

In the present edition the Ayres are scored for voice and piano, and while they could not have been presented in this way during the sixteenth century, their beauty will not be lost when so performed. Using modern instruments, the closest one could come to an Elizabethan performance would be to accompany the voice with guitar and 'cello. The guitar would have to play our piano part, which was originally written for the lute, and the 'cello would play the bass line of our piano score, which corresponds very closely to the bass viol part in the original. A performance in which a string trio or quartet played the various voices in the piano part would come very close to an Elizabethan performance for "Voyce and Viols." And there is nothing wrong with a purely instrumental rendition on either ancient or modern instruments since this, too, was sixteenth-century practice. Dowland's *Can She Excuse* and *Flow my Tears* both appear practically unaltered in instrumental collections as dances, the first a Galliard, the second a Pavane.

The first modern editions of Elizabethan music appeared in England in the middle of the nineteenth century after two hundred years of neglect. The names of Dowland, Morley, Campian were all but forgotten by 1650. It was not until the twentieth century that a truly representative body of this music was made available under the editorship of the English scholar, Dr. Edmund H. Fellowes. This made it possible at last for musicians to acquaint themselves with the great works of Tudor and Elizabethan times.

Our present collection includes some madrigals by Morley and Wilbye and some rounds and part-songs taken from the David Melvill *Booke of Roundels,* but most of the compositions were chosen from the thirty-odd books of Ayres published in London between 1597 and 1622. With the exception of the pieces from Melvill's MSS,* they were prepared from their original editions, and our edition maintains the original keys and note-values. The lute part, originally written in tablature, I have transcribed literally for the piano. There is no way of precisely indicating voice leading in tablature notation, but I have attempted to use the voice leading which seemed most natural. All the dynamic and tempo indications are my own; these, since there are none in the original, should be regarded merely as suggestions. Where I found what seemed to be an error, I gave the original indication in footnote. The added accidentals and modern metrical signatures are in brackets. I have retained the bar lines that appear in the original. The bar line as used in the sixteenth century has little relation to its later use and should be regarded essentially as an organizational device. It was employed primarily in music that appeared in score, such as the Ayres in which the lute tablature was directly under the solo voice part. Most often it appeared at irregular intervals. It rarely, however, conflicted with the basic metrical pattern. For example: in a triple meter (half

* Roxburghe Club, privately printed, 1916.

The Music

note getting one beat) the bar line would appear every six or nine beats rather than every three; in duple meter (half note getting one beat) it would be used every two, four, six, eight, or sixteen beats. Since it would be difficult for the modern reader to make metrical sense out of a "measure" consisting of eight, nine, or sixteen beats, I have thought it best to insert dotted bar lines at regular intervals which conform to the meter indicated by the composer. These, too, should be regarded as guide lines and are not intended to indicate stressed beats. The dotted bar lines are not meant to conflict in any way with the short rhythmic patterns that run counter to the meter in all Renaissance music.

We are deeply indebted to the authorities of the Folger Shakespeare Library, Washington, D.C.; the Huntington Library, San Marino, California; the Royal College of Music, London; and most especially to the British Museum, London, for so kindly placing at our disposal the original editions on which our own is based. We are also grateful to Mr. Joel Newman for his helpful suggestions concerning certain musicological problems.

Noah Greenberg

(Note: Some of the songs in this collection may be heard on the Columbia record, "An Evening of Elizabethan Verse and Its Music," performed by members of the New York Pro Musica Antiqua under the direction of Noah Greenberg.)

AN ANTHOLOGY OF
ELIZABETHAN LUTE SONGS,
MADRIGALS,
AND ROUNDS

SWEET WAS THE SONG

JOHN ATTEY

THE FIRST BOOK OF AYRES 1622

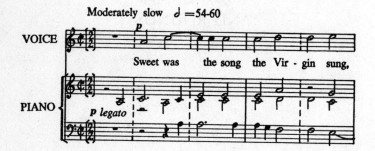

Sweet was the song the Vir - gin sung,

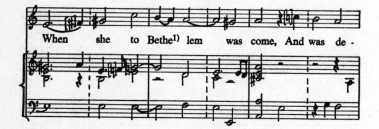

When she to Bethe[1] lem was come, And was de -

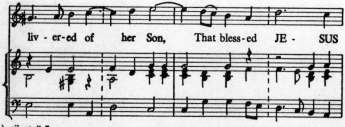

liv - er - ed of her Son, That bless - ed JE - SUS

1) silent "e"

2

hath to name, Lul- la ,lul-la, lul - la - by,

Lul- la, Lul-la, Lul-la —— by sweet Babe quoth

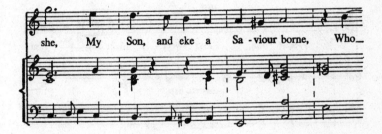

she, My Son, and eke a Sa - viour borne, Who—

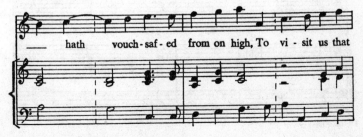

— hath vouch-saf - ed from on high, To vi - sit us that

were for - lorne, Lul - la, lul - la, lul-la - by, sweet

Babe sang she, And sweet -ly rockt him, rockt him,

rockt him, and sweet - ly rockt———— him,

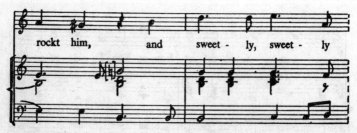

rockt him, and sweet - ly, sweet - ly

1) original: 𝅝

4

rockt   him   on   her————————   knee.

Sweet was the song the Virgin sung,
When she to Bethelem was come,
And was delivered of her Son,
That blessed JESUS hath to name,
        Lullaby,
Lullaby sweet Babe quoth she,
My Son, and eke a Saviour borne,
Who hath vouchsafed from on high,
To visit us that were forlorne,
        Lulla, Lulla,
Lullaby, sweet Babe sang she,
And sweetly rockt him, rockt him, rockt him,
And sweetly rockt him on her knee.

                                        ANONYMOUS

IF EVER HAPLES WOMAN

JOHN BARTLET

A BOOKE OF AYRES 1606

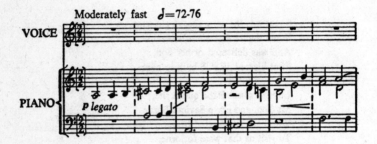

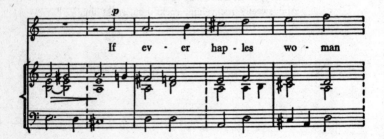

If ev - er hap - les wo - man had a cause To breath her plaintes in -

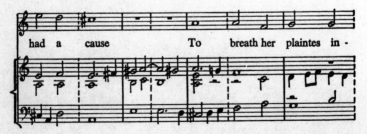

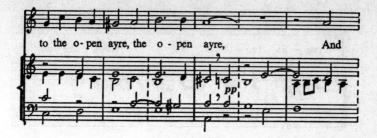

to the o-pen ayre, the o-pen ayre, And

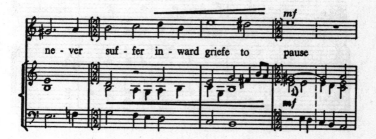

ne-ver suf-fer in-ward griefe to pause

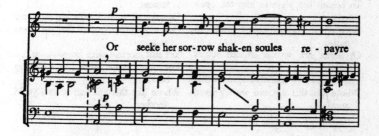

Or seeke her sor-row shak-en soules re-payre

Then I for I have lost my

1) original: ♩

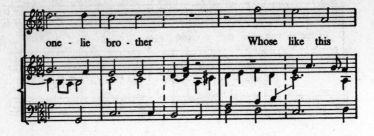

one - lie bro - ther   Whose like this

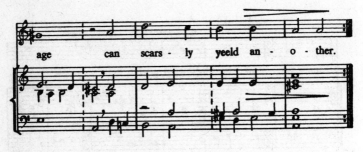

age   can   scars - ly   yeeld an - o - ther.

1

If ever haples woman had a cause
To breath her plaintes into the open
  ayre,
And never suffer inward griefe to
  pause
Or seeke her sorrow shaken soules
  repayre
Then I for I have lost my onelie brother
Whose like this age can scarsly yeeld
  another.

2

Come therefore mournefull Muses and
  lament,
Forsake all wanton pleasing motions,
Bedew your cheekes, stil shal my teares
  be spent:
Yet still increast with inundations,
For I must weepe, since I have lost my
  brother,
Whose like this age can scarsly yeeld
  another.

3

The cruell hand of murther cloyde
  with bloud
Lewdly deprivde him of his mortall
  life:
Woe the death attended blades that
  stoode,
In opposition gainst him in the strife,
Wherein he fell, and where I lost a
  brother,
Whose like this age can scarsly yeeld
  another.

4

Then unto griefe let me a Temple
  make,
And mourning dayly, enter sorrowes
  portes,
Knocke on my breast, sweete brother
  for thy sake,
Nature and Love will both be my
  consorts,
And helpe me aye to wayle my onely
  brother,
Whose like this age can scarsly yeeld
  another.

MARY, COUNTESS OF PEMBROOKE

OF ALL THE BIRDS

JOHN BARTLET   A BOOKE OF AYRES 1606

Of all the birds that I doe know,
For sit she high or sit shee

know, Phil - ip my spar - row hath no peer,
lowe, Be she far off or bee she neere

1)

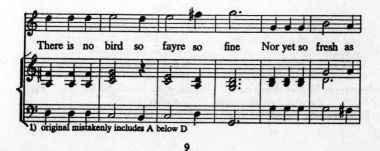

There is no bird so fayre so fine Nor yet so fresh as

1) original mistakenly includes A below D

9

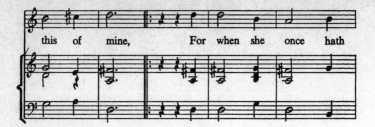

this of mine, For when she once hath

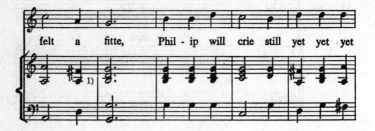

felt a fitte, Phil - ip will crie still yet yet yet

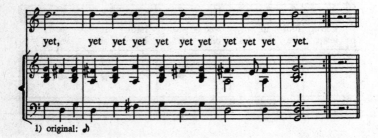

yet, yet yet yet yet yet yet yet yet yet yet.

1) original: ♪

Of all the birds that I doe know
Philip my sparrow hath no peer,
For sit she high or sit shee lowe,
Be she far off or bee she neere
There is no bird so fayre so fine
Nor yet so fresh as this of mine,
For when she once hath felt a fitte,
Philip will crie still yet yet yet.

Come in a morning merily,
When Philip hath been latelie fed,
Or in an Evening soberlie,
When Philip list to go to bed,
It is a heaven to heare my Phippe,
How she can chirpe with merry lippe,
For when, *etc.*

She never wanders far abroad;
But is at home when I do call,
If I command she laies on loade,*
With lips, with teeth, with tong and all,
She chaunts, she cherpes, she makes
    such cheare,
That I beleeve she hath no peere,
For when, *etc.*

And yet besides all this good sport,
My Philip can both sing and daunce,
With new found toyes of sundrie sort,
My Philip can both pricke and praunce.

And if you say but fend cut† Phippe,
Lord how the peate‡ wil turne and
    skippe,
For when, *etc.*

And to tel truth he were to blame,
Having so fine a bird as she,
To make him all this goodly game,
Without suspect or jelousie,
He were a churle, and knew no good,
Would see her faint for lacke of food.
For when, *etc.*

GEORGE GASCOIGNE

* *laies on loade:* "lays it on."
† *fend cut:* parry a thrust.
‡ *peate:* pet.

WHITHER RUNETH MY SWEETHART

JOHN BARTLET
A BOOKE OF AYRES 1606

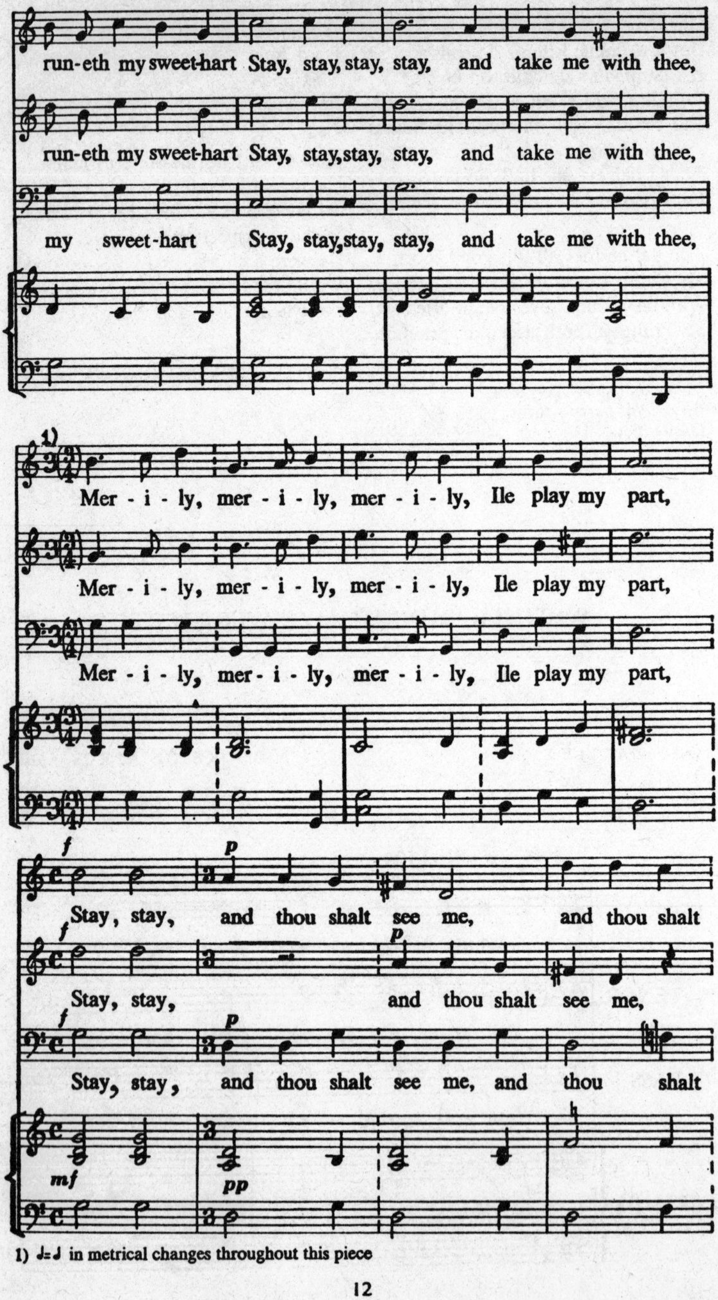

1) 𝅗𝅥=♩ in metrical changes throughout this piece

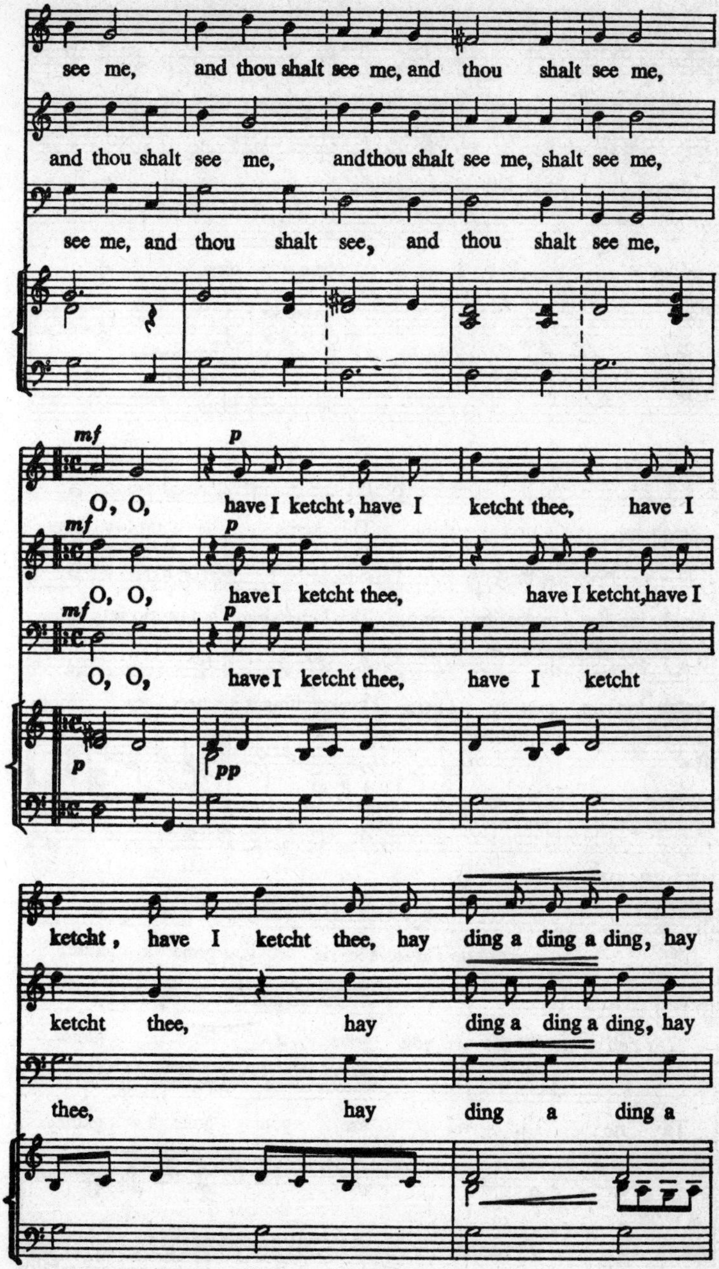

see me, and thou shalt see me, and thou shalt see me,

and thou shalt see me, and thou shalt see me, shalt see me,

see me, and thou shalt see, and thou shalt see me,

mf *p*

O, O, have I ketcht, have I ketcht thee, have I

mf *p*

O, O, have I ketcht thee, have I ketcht, have I

mf *p*

O, O, have I ketcht thee, have I ketcht

p *pp*

ketcht, have I ketcht thee, hay ding a ding a ding, hay

ketcht thee, hay ding a ding a ding, hay

thee, hay ding a ding a

ding a ding a ding, hay ding a ding a ding, hay ding a ding a ding, this

ding a ding a ding, hay ding a ding a ding, hay ding a ding a ding, this

ding   hay ding a   ding a   ding,   this

ketch-ing is   a pret-y thing, This ketch-ing   is a pret-y thing.

ketch-ing is a   prety prety thing,   This ketch-ing   is a prety prety thing.

ketch-ing is a   pret-ty   thing. This ketching is a   pret-ty   thing.

THE SECOND PART

Tar-rie Tar-rie Tar-rie are you gone a - gaine,

Tar-rieTar-rie Tar-rie are you   gone   a -   gaine,

Tar - rie   Tar - rie   are   you   gone a - gaine,

14

What no long-er lik - ing, I wil ketch thee once a - gaine,

What no long - er lik - ing, I wil ketch thee once a - gaine,

What no long - er lik - ing, I wil ketch thee once a - gaine,

I wil ketch thee once a - gaine, Stay while

I wil ketch thee once a - gaine, Stay while

I wil ketch thee once a - gaine, Stay while

I am ris - ing, stay while I am ris - ing, Do you tar -

I am ris - ing, while I am ris - ing, Do you tar -

I am ris - ing, while I am ris - ing, Do you tar -

ry   then pret-y lit-tle one, then pret-y lit-tle one,

ry   then pret-y lit-tle one, then pret-y lit-tle one,

ry then pret-y lit-tle one,   then pret-y lit tle one, then pret - y

then pret-y lit-tle   one, then pret-y lit-tle one, pret-y one pret-y one

then pret-y lit-tle   one, then pret-y lit-tle one, pret-y one pret-y one

lit- tle one,   then   pret - y   lit - tle one, pret-y one

mp (repeat pp)

I   thought   I   shold please thee   ere   we did

mp (repeat pp)

I thought   I   shold please thee   ere   we did part,

mp (repeat pp)

I   thought   I   shold please   thee   ere

p (repeat pp)

1) original: D, conflicts with bass part

16

part, ere we did ——————— part.

ere we did part.

that we did ——————— part.

Whither runeth my sweethart
Stay and take me with thee,
Merily Ile play my part,
Stay and thou shalt see me,
O have I ketcht thee, hay ding a ding a ding
This ketching is a prety thing.

Tarrie are you gone againe
What no longer liking,
I wil ketch thee once a-gaine,
Stay while I am rising,
Do you tarry then prety little one I
    thought
I shold please thee ere we did part.

ANONYMOUS

17

I CARE NOT FOR THESE LADIES

THOMAS CAMPIAN

PHILIP ROSSETER'S
A BOOKE OF AYRES 1601

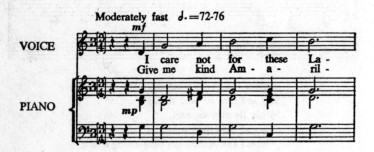

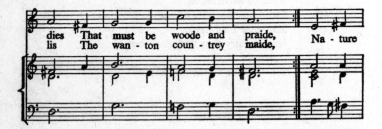

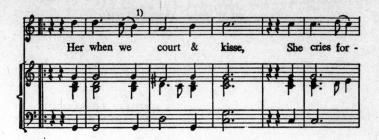

Her when we court & kisse, She cries for-

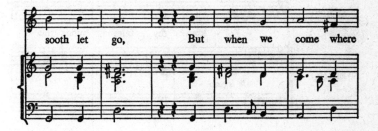

sooth let go, But when we come where

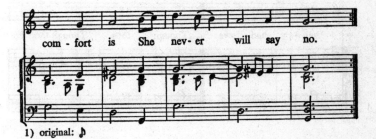

com-fort is She nev-er will say no.

1) original: ♪

2

If I love Amarillis,
She gives me fruit and flowers,
But if we love these Ladies,
We must give golden showers,
Give them gold that sell love,
Give me the Nutbrowne lasse,
  Who when we court, &c.

3

These Ladies must have pillowes,
And beds by strangers wrought,
Give me a Bower of willowes,
Of mosse and leaves unbought,
And fresh Amarillis
With milke and honie fed,
  Who when we court, &c.

THOMAS CAMPIAN

FOLLOWE THY FAIRE SUNNE

THOMAS CAMPIAN

PHILIP ROSSETER'S
A BOOKE OF AYRES 1601

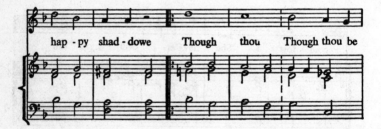

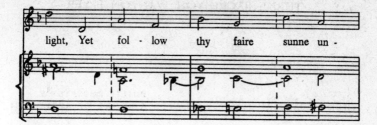

light, Yet fol - low thy faire sunne un -

hap ———— pie shad ———— dowe.

1

Followe thy faire sunne unhappy
    shaddowe
Though thou be blacke as night
And she made all of light,
Yet follow thy faire sunne unhappie
    shaddowe.

2

Follow her whose light thy light
    depriveth,
Though here thou liv'st disgrac't,
And she in heaven is plac't,
Yet follow her whose light the world
    reviveth.

3

Follow those pure beames whose
    beautie burneth
That so have scorched thee,
As thou still blacke must bee,
Til her kind beames thy black to
    brightness turneth.

4

Follow her while yet her glorie
    shineth:
There comes a luckless night,
That will dim all her light,
And this the black unhappie shade
    devineth.

5

Follow still since so thy fates ordained,
The Sunne must have his shade,
Till both at once do fade,
The Sun still prov'd* the shadow still
    disdained.

*prov'd: approved

THOMAS CAMPIAN

TURNE BACKE YOU WANTON FLYER

THOMAS CAMPIAN

PHILIP ROSSETER'S
A BOOKE OF AYRES 1601

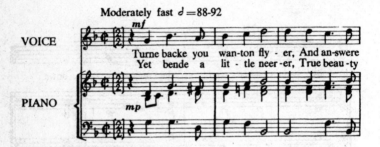

Turne backe you wan-ton fly - er, And an-swere
Yet bende a lit - tle neer -er, True beau -ty

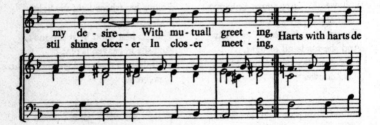

my de - sire —— With mu - tuall greet - ing, Harts with harts de
stil shines cleer - er In clos - er meet - ing,

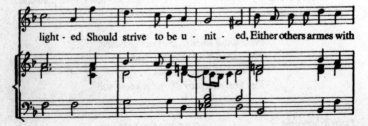

light - ed Should strive to be u - nit - ed, Either others armes with

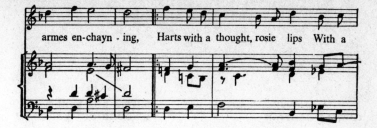

armes en-chayn - ing, Harts with a thought, rosie lips With a

kisse still en - ter tain - ing.

1

Turne backe you wanton flyer,
And answere my desire
With mutuall greeting,
Yet bende a little neerer,
True beauty stil shines cleerer
In closer meeting,
Harts with harts delighted
Should strive to be united,
Either others armes with armes
    enchayning,
Harts with a thought, rosie lips
With a kisse still entertaining.

2

What harvest halfe so sweete is
As still to reape the kisses
Growne ripe in sowing,
And straight to be receiver,
Of that which thou art giver,
Rich in bestowing.
There's no strickt observing,
Of times, or seasons changing,
There is ever one fresh spring abiding,
Then what we sow with our lips
Let us reape loves gaines deviding.

THOMAS CAMPIAN

FOLLOW YOUR SAINT

THOMAS CAMPIAN

PHILIP ROSSETER'S
A BOOKE OF AYRES 1601

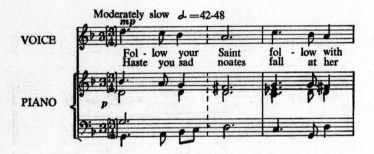

Moderately slow ♩. = 42-48

VOICE

Fol - low your Saint fol - low with
Haste you sad noates fall at her

PIANO

ac - cents sweet, There wrapt in cloud of
fly - ing feete, But if she scorns my

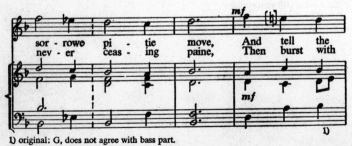

sor - rowe pi - tie move, And tell the
nev - er ceas - ing paine, Then burst with

1) original: G, does not agree with bass part.

24

rav - ish - er of my soule, I and
sigh - ing in her sight,

per - ish for her love.
nere re - turne a - gaine.

1

Follow your Saint follow with accents sweet,
Haste you sad noates fall at her flying feete,
There wrapt in cloud of sorrow pitie move,
And tell the ravisher of my soule, I perish for her love.
But if she scorns my never ceasing paine,
Then burst with sighing in her sight, and nere returne againe.

2

All that I soong still to her praise did tend,
Still she was first, still she my songs did end,
Yet she my love, and Musicke both doeth flie,
The Musicke that her Eccho is, and beauties simpathie;
Then let my Noates pursue her scornfull flight,
It shall suffice, that they were breath'd and dyed for her delight.

THOMAS CAMPIAN

53

FAIRE, IF YOU EXPECT ADMIRING

THOMAS CAMPIAN

PHILIP ROSSETER'S
A BOOKE OF AYRES 1601

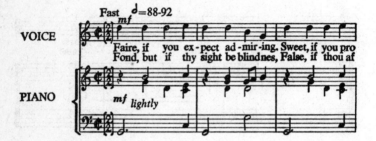

Faire, if you ex-pect ad-mir-ing. Sweet, if you pro
Fond, but if thy sight be blindnes, False, if thou af

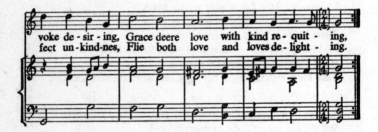

voke de-sir-ing, Grace deere love with kind re-quit-ing,
fect un-kind-nes, Flie both love and loves de-light-ing.

Then when hope is lost and love is scorn-ed,

Ile bu-ry my de - sires, and quench the fires that

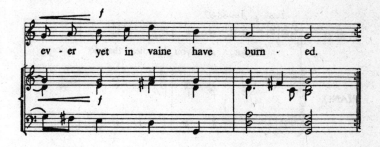

ev - er yet in vaine have burn · ed.

1

Faire, if you expect admiring,
Sweet, if you provoke desiring,
Grace deere love with kind requiting,
Fond, but if thy sight be blindnes,
False, if thou affect unkindnes,
Flie both love and loves delighting.
Then when hope is lost and love is scorned,
Ile bury my desires, and quench the fires that ever yet in vaine have burned.

2

Fates, if you rule lovers fortune,
Stars, if men your powers importune,
Yield reliefe by your relenting:
Time, if sorrow be not endles,
Hope made vaine, and pittie friendles,
Helpe to ease my long lamenting.
But if griefes remaine still unredressed,
Ile flie to her againe, and sue for pitie to renue my hopes distressed.

THOMAS CAMPIAN

27

HARKE AL YOU LADIES

THOMAS CAMPIAN

PHILIP ROSSETER'S
A BOOKE OF AYRES 1601

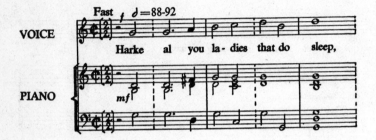

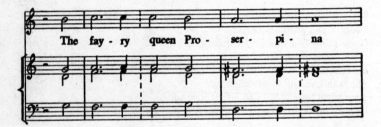

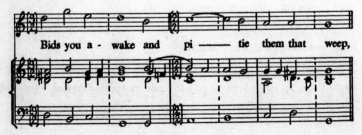

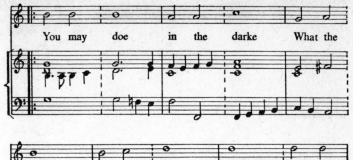

You may doe in the darke What the

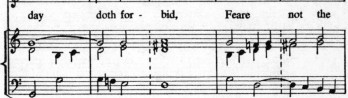

day doth for - bid, Feare not the

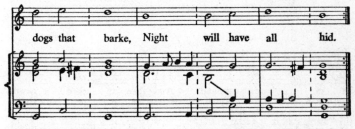

dogs that barke, Night will have all hid.

2

But if you let your lovers mone,
  The Fairie Queene Proserpina
Will send abroad her Fairies ev'ry one,
  That shall pinch blacke and blew,
Your white hands, and faire armes,
  That did not kindly rue
        Your Paramours harmes.

4

All you that will hold watch with love,
  The Fairie Queene Proserpina,
Will make you fairer than Diones
  dove,
  Roses red, Lillies white,
And the cleare damaske hue
  Shall on your cheekes alight,
        Love will adorne you.

3

In Myrtle Arbours on the downes,
  The Fairie Queene Proserpina,
This night by moone-shine leading
  merrie rounds,
  Holds a watch with sweet love,
Downe the dale, up the hill,
  No plaints or groanes may move
        Their holy vigill.

5

All you that love, or lov'd before,
  The Fairie Queene Proserpina
Bids you encrease that loving
  humour more,
  They that yet have not fed
On delight amorous,
  She vowes that they shall lead
        Apes in Avernus.

THOMAS CAMPIAN

WHEN THOU MUST HOME

THOMAS CAMPIAN

PHILIP ROSSETER'S
A BOOKE OF AYRES 1601

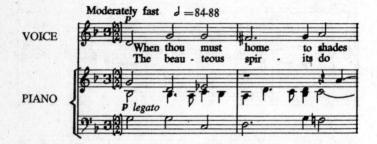

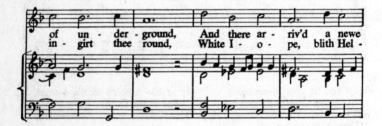

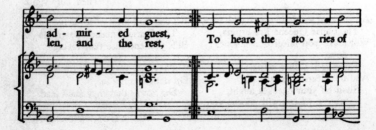

thy fin - isht love, From that smoothe

toong whose mu - sicke hell can move.

1

When thou must home to shades of under ground,
And there arriv'd a newe admired guest,
The beauteous spirits do ingirt thee round,
White Iope, blith Hellen, and the rest,
To heare the stories of thy finisht love,
From that smoothe toong whose musicke hell can move.

2

Then wilt thou speake of banqueting delights,
Of masks and revels which sweete youth did make,
Of Turnies and great challenges of knights,
And all these triumphes for thy beauties sake,
When thou hast told these honours done to thee,
Then tell, O tell how thou didst murther me.

THOMAS CAMPIAN

NEVER WEATHER-BEATEN SAILE

TWO BOOKES OF AYRES
THE FIRST BOOK 1613

THOMAS CAMPIAN

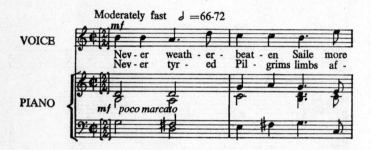

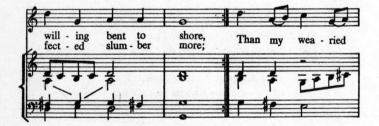

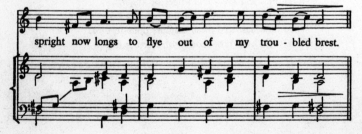

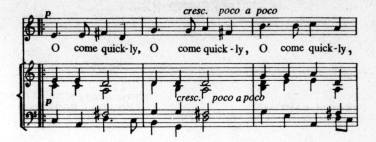

O come quick-ly, O come quick-ly, O come quick-ly,

sweet - est Lord, and take my soule to rest.

1) use fermata at end of full verse.

1

Never weather-beaten Saile more willing bent to shore,
Never tyred Pilgrims limbs affected slumber more;
Than my wearied spright now longs to flye out of my troubled brest:
    O come quickly sweetest Lord, and take my soule to rest.

2

Ever blooming are the joyes of Heav'ns high paradice,
Cold age deafes not there our eares, nor vapour dims our eyes;
Glory there the Sun outshines, whose beames the blessed onely see:
    O come quickly glorious Lord, and raise my spright to thee.

THOMAS CAMPIAN

JACKE AND JONE

THOMAS CAMPIAN

TWO BOOKES OF AYRES
THE FIRST BOOK 1613

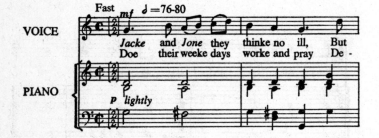

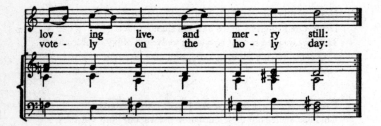

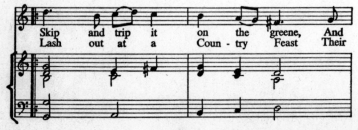

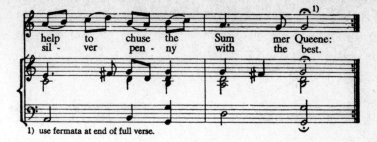

help   to   chuse   the   Sum   mer Queene:
sil - ver   pen - ny   with   the best.

1) use fermata at end of full verse.

1

Jacke and *Jone* they thinke no ill,
But loving live, and merry still:
Doe their weeke days worke and pray
Devotely on the holy day:
Skip and trip it on the greene,
And help to chuse the Summer
    Queene:
Lash out at a Country Feast
Their silver penny with the best.

2

Well can they judge of nappy Ale
And tell at large a Winter tale:
Climbe up to the Apple loft,
And turne the Crabs till they be soft.
Tib is all the fathers joy,
And little *Tom* the mothers boy:
All their pleasure is content,
And care to pay their yearely rent.

3

Jone can call by name her Cowes,
And decke her windowes with
    greene boughs,
Shee can wreathes and tuttyes* make,
And trimme with plums a Bridall
    Cake.
Jacke knowes what brings gaine
    or losse,
And his long Flaile can stoutly tosse,
Make the hedge which others breake,
And ever thinkes what he doth
    speake.

* *tuttyes:* nosegays.

4

Now you Courtly Dames and Knights,
That study onely strange delights,
Though you scorne the home-spun
    gray,
And revell in your rich array,
Though your tongues dissemble
    deepe,
And can your heads from danger
    keepe;
Yet for all your pompe and traine,
Securer lives the silly Swaine.

THOMAS CAMPIAN

ALL LOOKES BE PALE

THOMAS CAMPIAN

TWO BOOKES OF AYRES
THE FIRST BOOK 1613

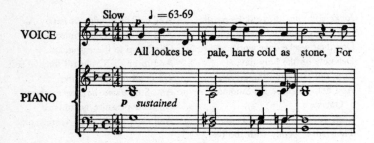

All lookes be pale, harts cold as stone, For

Hal-ly now is dead, and gone, Hal —— ly in whose sight,

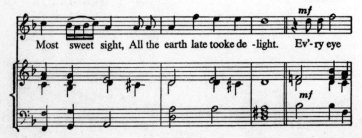

Most sweet sight, All the earth late tooke de -light. Ev'-ry eye

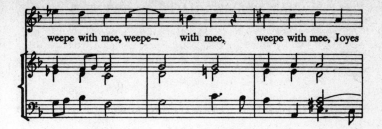

weepe with mee, weepe— with mee, weepe with mee, Joyes

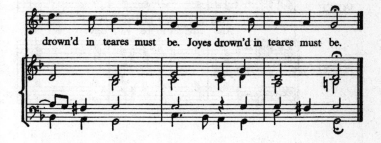

drown'd in teares must be. Joyes drown'd in teares must be.

1

All lookes be pale, harts cold as stone,
For *Hally* now is dead, and gone,
    Hally in whose sight,
    Most sweet sight,
    All the earth late tooke delight.
Ev'ry eye weepe with mee,
Joyes drown'd in teares must be.

2

His Iv'ry skin, his comely hayre,
His Rosie cheekes, so cleare,
    and faire:
        Eyes that once did grace
        His bright face,
        Now in him all want their
        place.
Eyes and hearts weepe with mee,
For who so kinde as hee?

3

His youth was like an *Aprill* flowre,
Adorn'd with beauty, love, and
    powre,
    Glory strow'd his way,
    Whose wreaths gay
    Now are all turn'd to decay.
Then againe weepe with mee,
None feele more cause than wee.

4

No more may his wisht sight returne,
His golden Lampe no more can
    burne;
        Quenched is all his flame,
        His hop't fame
        Now hath left him nought
        but name.
For him all weepe with mee,
Since more him none shall see.

THOMAS CAMPIAN

37

WHAT HARVEST HALFE SO SWEET IS

THOMAS CAMPIAN   THE SECOND BOOKE OF AYRES 1613

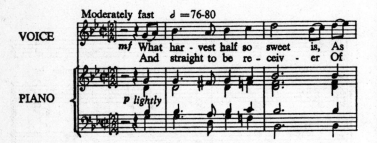

Moderately fast ♩=76-80

VOICE

mf What har-vest half so sweet is, As
And straight to be re-ceiv-er Of

PIANO

p lightly

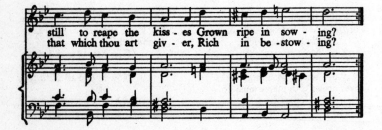

still to reape the kiss-es Grown ripe in sow-ing?
that which thou art giv-er, Rich in be-stow-ing?

Kiss then, my har-vest Queene, Full

1)

1) original: E♭

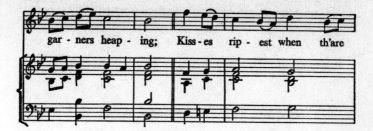

gar-ners heap-ing; Kiss-es rip-est when th'are

greene, Want one-ly reap-ing. -ing.

1

What harvest half so sweet is,
As still to reape the kisses
  Grown ripe in sowing?
And straight to be receiver
Of that which thou art giver,
  Rich in bestowing?
Kiss then, my harvest Queene,
  Full garners heaping;
Kisses ripest when th' are greene,
  Want onely reaping.

2

The Dove alone expresses
Her fervencie in kisses,
  Of all most loving:
A creature as offencelesse,
As those things that are sencelesse,
  And void of moving.
Let us so love and kisse,
  Though all envie us:
That which kinde, and harmlesse is,
  None can denie us.

THOMAS CAMPIAN

THOMAS CAMPIAN

THE SECOND BOOKE OF AYRES 1613

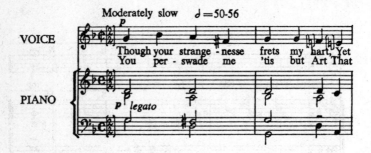

Though your strange - nesse frets my hart, Yet
You per - swade me 'tis but Art That

may not I com - plaine:
se - cret love must faine.
If an - oth - er

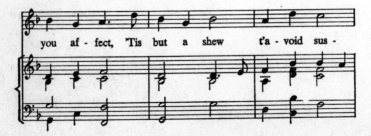

you af - fect, 'Tis but a shew t'a - void sus -

pect, Is this faire ex-

cus- ing? O no, all is a - bus - ing.

1) original: 𝅘𝅥𝅭

1

Though your strangenesse frets my
   hart,
Yet may not I complaine:
You perswade me 'tis but Art
That secret love must faine.
If another you affect,
'Tis but a shew t'avoid suspect,
Is this faire excusing? O no, all is
   abusing.

2

Your wisht sight if I desire,
Suspitions you pretend,
Causelesse you your selfe retire
While I in vain attend:
This a Lover whets you say,
Still made more eager by delay.
Is this faire excusing? O no, all is
   abusing.

3

When another holds your hand,
You sweare I hold your hart:
When my Rivals close doe stand,
And I sit farre apart,
I am neerer yet than they,
Hid in your bosome, as you say.
Is this faire excusing? O no, all is
   abusing.

4

Would my Rival then I were,
Or els your secret friend:
So much lesser should I feare,
And not so much attend.
They enjoy you ev'ry one,
Yet I must seeme your friend alone.
Is this faire excusing? O no, all is
   abusing.

THOMAS CAMPIAN

KINDE ARE HER ANSWERES

THOMAS CAMPIAN   THE THIRD BOOKE OF AYRES 1617

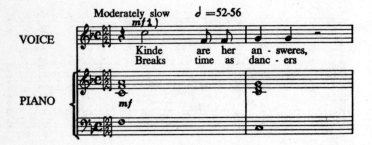

Kinde   are   her   an - sweres,
Breaks   time   as   danc - ers

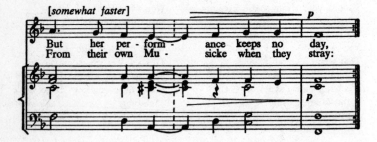

[somewhat faster]

But   her   per - form -   ance   keeps   no   day,
From   their own   Mu -   sicke   when   they   stray:

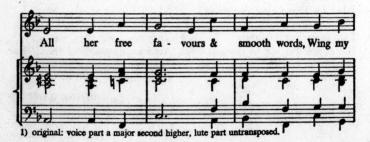

All   her   free   fa - vours &   smooth words, Wing my

1) original: voice part a major second higher, lute part untransposed.

42

2) use fermata at end of full verse.

1

Kinde are her answeres,
    But her performance keeps no day,
Breaks time as dancers
    From their own Musicke when they
    stray:
    All her free favours & smooth
    words,
Wing my hopes in vaine.
O did ever voice so sweet but only
    fain?
    Can true love yeeld such delay,
    Converting joy to pain?

2

Lost is our freedome,
    When we submit to women so:
Why doe we neede them,
    When in their best they worke our
    woe?
    There is no wisedome
Can altar ends by Fate prefixt;
O why is the good of man with evill
    mixt?
    Never were days yet cal'd two,
    But one night went betwixt.

THOMAS CAMPIAN

43

BREAKE NOW MY HEART AND DYE

THOMAS CAMPIAN   THE THIRD BOOKE OF AYRES 1617

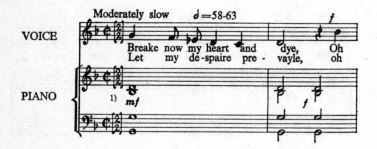

Breake now my heart and dye, Oh
Let my de-spaire pre-vayle, oh

no, oh no, she may re-lent.
stay, oh stay, hope is not spent.

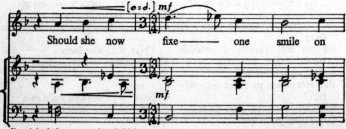

Should she now fixe—— one smile on

1) original: lute part a fourth higher.

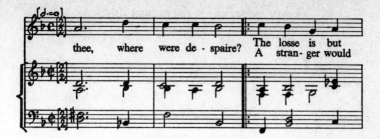

thee, where were de - spaire? The losse is but

A stran- ger would

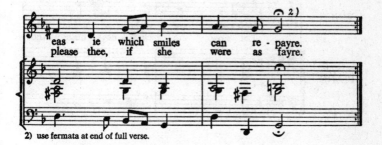

eas - ie which smiles can re - payre.
please thee, if she were as fayre.

2) use fermata at end of full verse.

1

Breake now my heart and dye, Oh no, she may relent.
Let my despaire prevayle, oh stay, hope is not spent.
Should she now fixe one smile on thee, where were despaire?
 The losse is but easie which smiles can repayre.
 A stranger would please thee, if she were as fayre.

2

Her must I love or none, so sweet none breathes as shee,
The more is my despayre, alas she loves not me:
But cannot time make way for love through ribs of steele?
 The Grecian inchanted all parts but the heele,
 At last a shafte daunted which his hart did feele.

THOMAS CAMPIAN

NOW WINTER NIGHTS ENLARGE

THOMAS CAMPIAN   THE THIRD BOOKE OF AYRES 1617

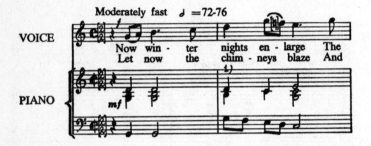

Now win - ter nights en - large The
Let now the chim - neys blaze And

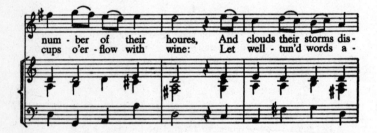

num - ber of their houres, And clouds their storms dis -
cups o'er - flow with wine: Let well - tun'd words a -

charge Up - on the ayr - ie towres, Now yel - low
maze With har - mo - nie di - vine.

1) original: E

46

wax-en lights Shall waite on hun-ny Love, While youthfull Revels,

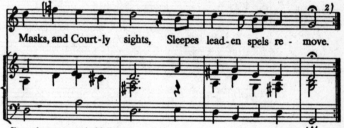

Masks, and Court-ly sights, Sleepes lead-en spels re - move.

2) use fermata at end of full verse.

1

Now winter nights enlarge
The number of their houres,
And clouds their storms discharge
Upon the ayrie towres,
Let now the chimneys blaze
And cups o'erflow with wine:
Let well-tun'd words amaze
With harmonie divine.
Now yellow waxen lights
Shall waite on hunny Love,
While youthfull Revels, Masks, and Courtly sights,
Sleepes leaden spels remove.

2

This time doth well dispence
With lovers long discourse;
Much speech hath some defence,
Though beauty no remorse.
All doe not all things well;
Some measures comely tread;
Some knotted Ridles tell;
Some Poems smoothly read.
The Summer hath his joyes,
And Winter his delights;
Though Love and all his pleasures are but toyes,
They shorten tedious nights.

THOMAS CAMPIAN

47

IF THOU LONGST SO MUCH TO LEARNE

THOMAS CAMPIAN THE THIRD BOOKE OF AYRES 1617

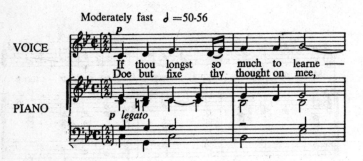

If thou longst so much to learne —
Doe but fixe thy thought on mee,

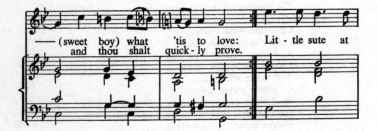

— (sweet boy) what 'tis to love:
and thou shalt quick-ly prove.
Lit - tle sute at

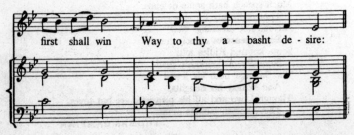

first shall win Way to thy a - basht de - sire:

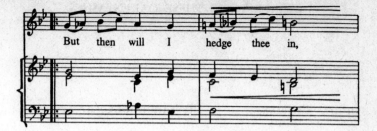

But then will I hedge thee in,

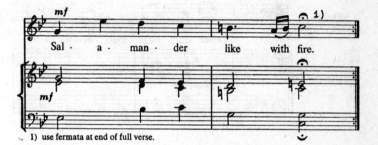

mf

Sal - a - man - der like with fire. 1)

1) use fermata at end of full verse.

1

If thou longst so much to learne (sweet
    boy) what 'tis to love:
Doe but fixe thy thought on mee, and
    thou shalt quickly prove.
    Little sute at first shall win
      Way to thy abasht desire:
    But then will I hedge thee in,
      Salamander-like with fire.

2

With thee dance I will, and sing, and
    thy fond dalliance beare;
Wee the grovy hils will climbe, and
    play the wantons there.
    Other whiles wee'le gather flowres,
      Lying dalying on the grasse,
    And thus our delightfull howres
      Full of waking dreames shall
      passe.

3

When thy joyes were thus at height my
    love should turne from thee,
Old acquaintance then should grow as
    strange as strange might be,
    Twenty rivals thou shouldst finde
      Breaking all their hearts for mee,
    When to all Ile prove more kinde,
      And more forward than to thee.

4

Thus thy silly youth enrag'd would
    soone my love defie;
But alas poore soule too late, clipt
    wings can never flye:
    Those sweet houres which wee had
      past
      Cal'd to mind thy heart would
      burne:
    And could'st thou flye ne'er so fast,
      They would make thee straight
      returne.

THOMAS CAMPIAN

THRICE TOSSE THESE OAKEN ASHES

THOMAS CAMPIAN   THE THIRD BOOKE OF AYRES 1617

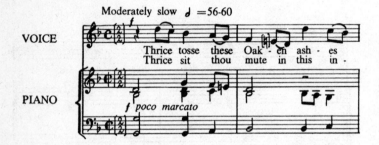

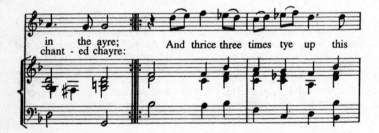

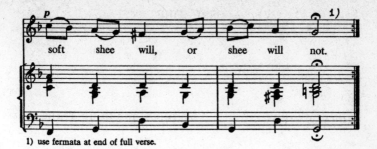

soft   shee   will,   or   shee   will   not.

1) use fermata at end of full verse.

1

Thrice tosse these Oaken ashes in the ayre;
Thrice sit thou mute in this inchanted chayre:
And thrice three times tye up this true loves knot,
And murmur soft shee will, or shee will not.

2

Goe burn these poys'nous weedes in yon blew fire,
These Screech-owles fethers, and this prickling bryer,
This Cypresse gathered at a dead mans grave;
That all thy feares and cares an end may have.

3

Then come you Fayries, dance with me a round,
Melt her hard hart with your melodious sound:
In vaine are all the charms I can devise,
She hath an Arte to breake them with her eyes.

THOMAS CAMPIAN

51

FIRE, FIRE

THOMAS CAMPIAN

THE THIRD BOOKE OF AYRES 1617

Fire, fire, fire, fire,

Loe here I burne   I burne   in such de- sire, That all

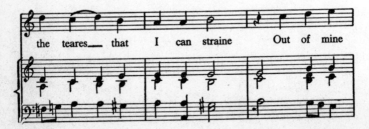

the teares___ that   I   can straine   Out   of   mine

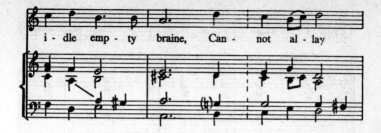

i - dle emp - ty braine, Can - not al - lay

my scorch - ing paine. Come *Trent* and

Hum - *ber*, and —— fayre *Thames*,

Dread O - cean haste with all —— thy

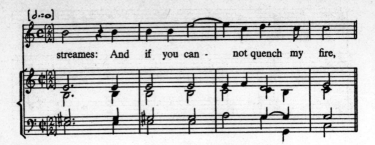

1) in the original there is a rest here which adds a beat to the voice part.

1

Fire, fire, fire, fire,
Loe here I burne in such desire,
That all the teares that I can straine
Out of mine idle empty braine,
Cannot allay my scorching paine.
    Come *Trent* and *Humber*, and fayre *Thames*,
    Dread Ocean haste with all thy streames:
    And if you cannot quench my fire,
    O drowne both mee, and my desire.

2

Fire, fire, fire, fire,
There is no hell to my desire:
See all the Rivers backward flye,
And th'Ocean doth his waves deny,
For feare my heate should drink them dry.
    Come heav'nly showres then pouring downe;
    Come you that once the world did drowne:
    Some then you spar'd, but now save all,
    That else must burne, and with mee fall.

THOMAS CAMPIAN

SILLY BOY, 'TIS FUL MOONE

THOMAS CAMPIAN   THE THIRD BOOKE OF AYRES 1617

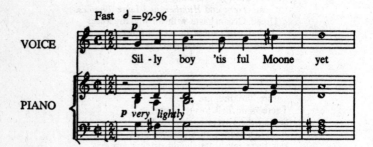

Sil - ly boy 'tis ful Moone yet

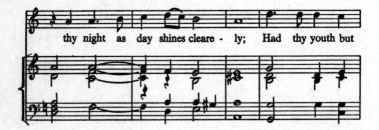

thy night as day shines cleare - ly; Had thy youth but

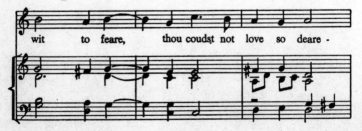

wit to feare, thou coudst not love so deare -

ly: Short - ly wilt thou mourne when all thy
pleas - ures are be - reav - ed; Lit tle knowes he how to
love that nev - er was de - ceiv - ed.

2
This is thy first mayden flame that tri-
umphes yet unstayned;
All is artless now you speake, not one
word yet is fayned;
All is heav'n that you behold, and all
your thoughts are blessed:
But no Spring can want his Fall, each
Troylus hath his *Cresseid*.

3
Thy well-order'd lockes ere long shall
rudely hang neglected;
And thy lively pleasant cheare, reade
griefe on earth dejected:

Much then wilt thou blame thy Saint
that made thy heart so holy,
And with sighs confesse, in love, that
too much faith is folly.

4
Yet be just and constant still, Love
may beget a wonder;
Not unlike a Summers frost, or Winters
fatall thunder:
He that holds his Sweet-hart true unto
his day of dying,
Lives of all that ever breath'd most
worthy the envying.

THOMAS CAMPIAN

57

SO QUICKE, SO HOT, SO MAD

THOMAS CAMPIAN   THE THIRD BOOKE OF AYRES 1617

So quicke, so hot, so
That faine I would with

mad is thy fond sute, So
losse make thy tongue mute, And

rude, so te-dious growne, in
yeeld some lit-tle grace, to

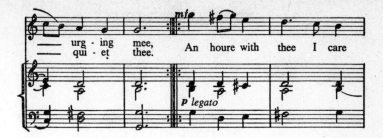

urg - ing mee,
qui - et thee.

An houre with thee I care

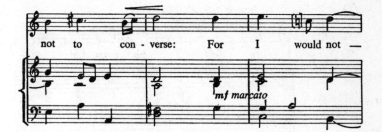

not to con - verse: For I would not —

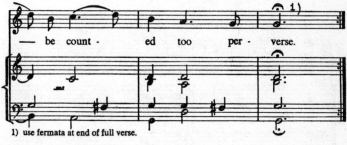

— be count - ed too per - verse.

1) use fermata at end of full verse.

2

But roofes too hot would prove for
    men all fire,
And hils too high for my unused pace;
The grove is charg'd with thornes and
    the bold bryer;
Gray Snakes the meadowes shrowde in
    every place:
  A yellow Frog, alas will fright me so
  As I should start and tremble as I
    goe.

3

Since then I can on earth no fit roome
    finde,
In heav'n I am resolv'd with you to
    meete;
Till then for Hopes sweet sake rest
    your tir'd mind,
And not so much as see mee in the
    streete
  A heavenly meeting one day wee
    shall have,
  But never, as you dreame, in bed, or
    grave.

THOMAS CAMPIAN

TO HIS SWEET LUTE

THOMAS CAMPIAN   THE FOURTH BOOKE OF AYRES 1617

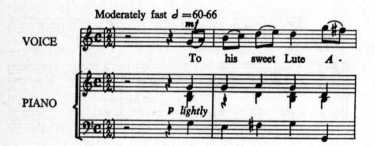

Moderately fast ♩ = 60-66

To his sweet Lute A-

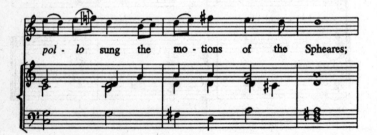

pol - lo sung the mo - tions of the Spheares;

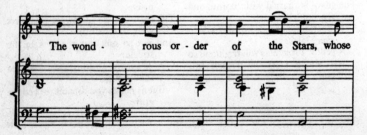

The wond - rous or - der of the Stars, whose

course di-vides the yeares: And all the Mys - ter - ies a - bove;

But none of this could *Mi - das* move, Which

pur - chast him his Ass - es eares.

2

Then *Pan* with his rude Pipe began the Country-wealth t'advance;
To boast of Cattle, flocks of Sheepe, and Goates, on hils that dance,
With much more of this churlish kinde:
That quite transported *Midas* minde,
And held him rapt as in a trance.

3

This wrong the *God of Musicke* scorned from such a sottish Judge,
And bent his angry bow at *Pan*, which made the Piper trudge:
Then *Midas* head he so did trim,
That ev'ry age yet talkes of him
And *Phoebus* right revenged grudge.

·THOMAS CAMPIAN

THINK'ST THOU TO SEDUCE ME THEN

THOMAS CAMPIAN   THE FOURTH BOOKE OF AYRES 1617

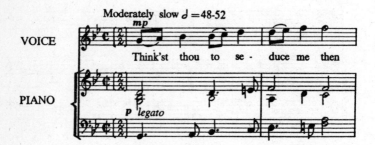

Think'st thou to se - duce me then

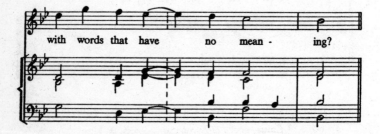

with words that have no mean - ing?

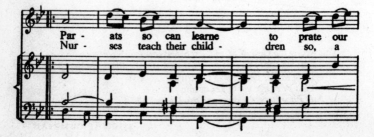

Par - ats so can learne to prate our
Nur - ses teach their child - dren so, a

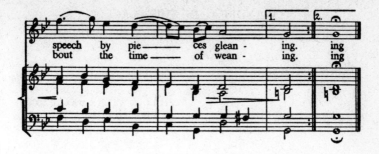

speech by pie——ces glean - ing.
bout the time—— of wean - ing.
ing
ing

1

Think's thou to seduce me then with words that have no meaning?
Parats so can learne to prate our speech by pieces gleaning.
Nurses teach their children so, about the time of weaning.

2

Learne to speake first, then to wooe, to wooing much pertayneth:
Hee that courts us wanting Arte, soon falters when he faineth:
Lookes a-squint on his discourse, and smiles when hee complaineth.

3

Skilfull Anglers hide their hookes, fit baytes for every season;
But with crooked pins fish thou, as babes that doe want reason,
Gogions* onely can be caught with such poore trickes of treason.

4

Ruth forgive me if I err'd from humane hearts compassion,
When I laught sometimes too much to see thy foolish fashion:
But alas, who lesse could doe that found so good occasion?

THOMAS CAMPIAN

*Gogions: Gudgeons.

WANDRING IN THIS PLACE

MICHAELL CAVENDISH

14 AYRES IN TABLETORIE
TO THE LUTE 1598

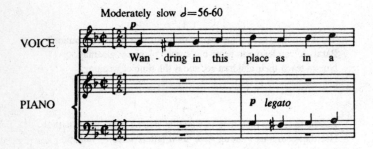

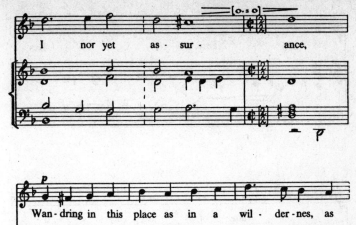

I nor yet as - sur - ance,

Wan - dring in this place as in a wil - der - nes, as

in a wil - der - nes, as in a wil - der -

nes, No com - fort have I nor yet

as - sur - ance, Des -

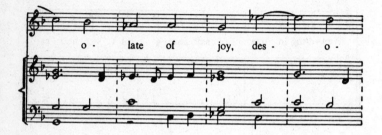

o - late of joy, des - o -

late of joy, des - o -

late of joy, des - o -

66

late of joy, re - pleat with sad - nesse:

Wher - fore I _____ may

say, O de - us, de - us,

Non est do - lor, sic - ut do - lor me - us,

non est do - lor, sic - ut

do lor, non est do - lor

sic - ut do - lor me ———— us.

Wandring in this place as in a wilderness,
No comfort have I nor yet assurance,
Desolate of joy, repleat with sadnesse:
Wherfore I may say, *O deus, deus,*
Non est dolor, sicut dolor meus.

ANONYMOUS

DOWN IN A VALLEY

MICHAELL CAVENDISH

14 AYRES IN TABLETORIE
TO THE LUTE 1598

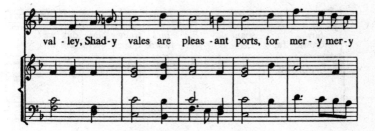

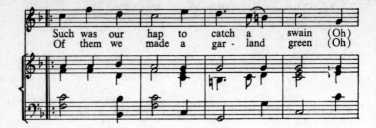

Such was our hap to catch a swain (Oh)
Of them we made a gar - land green (Oh)

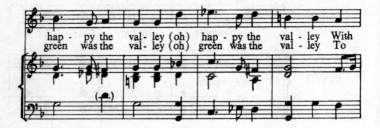

hap - py the val - ley (oh) hap - py the val - ley With
green was the val - ley (oh) green was the val - ley To

flowrs to span - gle *Flo - raes* traine, Nor did we
crown faire *Lel - ia* shep - heards queen, Faire as a

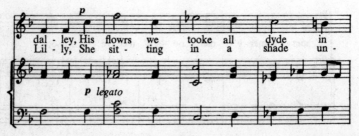

dal - ley, His flowrs we tooke all dyde in
Lil - ly, She sit - ting in a shade un -

graine. (Oh) dyde was the val-ley, Shad-y vales are
seene. (Oh) shad-ie the val-ley,

pleas-ant ports For mer-y mer-y

mer-y mer-y mer-y lads meet re-   sorts.

Down in a valley,
Shady vales are pleasant ports,
For mery lads meet resorts.
Such was our hap to catch a swain
    (Oh) happy the valley
With flowrs to spangle *Floraes* traine,
    Nor did we dalley,
His flowrs we tooke all dyde in graine*
    (Oh) dyde was the valley,
Shady vales are pleasant ports

For mery lads meet resorts.
Of them we made a garland green
    (Oh) green was the valley
To crown faire *Lelia* shepheards queen,
    Faire as a Lilly,
She sitting in a shade unseene.
    (Oh) shadie the valley,
Shady vales are pleasant ports
For mery lads meet resorts.

ANONYMOUS

*dyde in graine: forthrightly.

71

EVERIE BUSH NEW SPRINGING

14 AYRES IN TABLETORIE
TO THE LUTE 1598

MICHAELL CAVENDISH

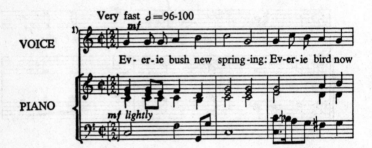

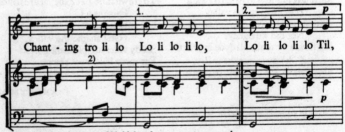

1) original: voice part a fifth higher, lute part untransposed.
2) original has barline here.

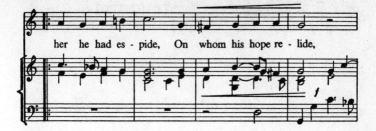

her he had es - pide, On whom his hope re - lide,

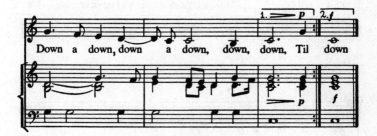

Down a down a down, Down with a frown Oh she puld him down.

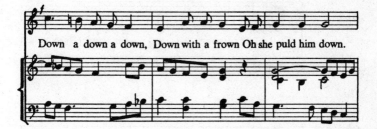

Down a down, down a down, down, down, Til down

Everie bush new springing:
Everie bird now singing,
Merily sate poore *Nico*
   Chanting tro li lo
   Lo li lo li lo
Til her he had espide,
On whom his hope relide,
   Down a down a down,
   Down with a frown
   Oh she puld him down.

ANONYMOUS

73

TWO LOVERS SAT LAMENTING

WILLIAM CORKINE   THE SECOND BOOKE OF AYRES 1612

Moderately slow ♩ =50-54

VOICE

p legato

Two lov-ers sat la - ment-ing, Hard by a Cris - tall _____ brooke, Each oth-ers hart tor-ment-ing, Ex-chang-ing looke for looke, With sighes and teares be-wray-ing, Their si - lent thoughts de - lay-ing, At last coth one,

PIANO

[somewhat faster]

1) original scoring: voice and viola da gamba.

74

Shall we a lone, Sit here our thoughts be-wray-ing?

Fie, fie, fie, fie, fie, oh fie, it

may not be, Set look-ing by,

Let speak ing set us free.

2

Then thus their silence breaking
Their thoughts too long estranged
They do bewray by speaking,
And words with words exchanged:
　　Then one of them replyed
　　Great pity we had dyed,
　　Thus all alone
　　In silent moane
And not our thoughts descryed.
　　Fie, fie, oh fie,
Oh fie, that had beene ill
　　That inwardly
Sylence the hart should kill.

3

From lookes and words to kisses
They made their next proceeding,
And as their onely blisses
They therein were exceeding.
　　Oh what a joy is this,
　　To looke, to talke, to kisse?
　　But thus begunne
　　Is all now done?
Ah: all then nothing is.
　　Fie, fie, oh fie,
Oh fie, it is a Hell
　　And better dye
Than kisse, and not end well.

ANONYMOUS

TYME CRUELL TYME

JOHN DANYEL   SONGS FOR THE LUTE VIOL AND VOICE 1606

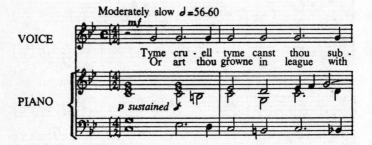

Tyme cru-ell tyme canst thou sub-
Or art thou growne in league with

due that brow those faire eyes, That con- quers
those faire eyes, That they might

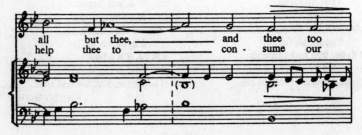

all but thee, _____ and thee too
help thee to _____ con- sume our

76

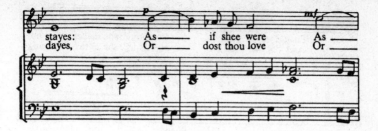

stayes: As ____ if shee were   As ____
dayes,   Or ____ dost thou love   Or ____

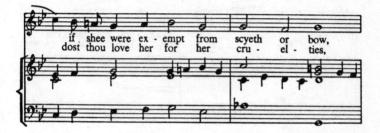

if shee were ex - empt from scyeth or bow,
dost thou love her for her cru - el - ties,

From Love and yeares un - sub - ject
Being mer - ci - lesse lyke thee that

to de - cayes?
no man wayes?

77

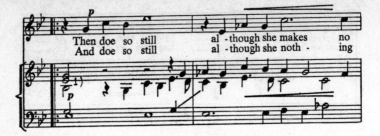

Then doe so still   al - though she makes   no
And doe so still   al - though she noth - ing

'steeme, Of dayes —— nor yeares, but lets them run in
cares, Doe as —— I doe,—— love her al - though un -

vaine: Hold still, —— thy swift wing'd
kinde, Hould still, —— yet O I

hours that won - dring seeme, To
feare at un - a - wares, Thou

1) original: D

78

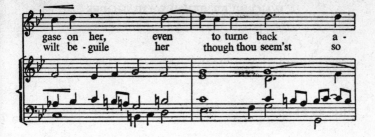

gase on her, even to turne back a -
wilt be-guile her though thou seem'st so

gaine, - gaine.
kinde, kinde.

1	2
Tyme cruell tyme canst thou subdue that brow	Or art thou growne in league with those faire eyes,
That conquers all but thee, and thee too stayes:	That they might help thee to consume our dayes,
As if shee were exempt from scyeth or bow,	Or dost thou love her for her cruelties,
From Love and yeares unsubject to decayes.	Being mercilesse lyke thee that no man wayes?

3	4
Then doe so still although she makes no 'steeme	And doe so still although she nothing cares,
Of dayes nor yeares, but lets them run in vaine:	Doe as I doe, love her although un-kinde,
Hold still thy swift wing'd hours that wondring seeme	Hould still, yet O I feare at unawares,
To gase on her, even to turne back againe.	Thou wilt beguile her though thou seem'st so kinde.

SAMUEL DANIEL

79

JOHN DOWLAND   THE FIRST BOOKE OF SONGES 1597
₁₎

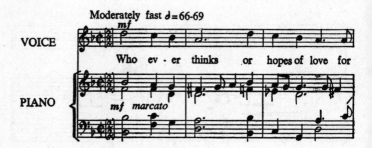

Who ev - er thinks or hopes of love for

love, Or who be - lov'd in *Cu - pids* lawes doth

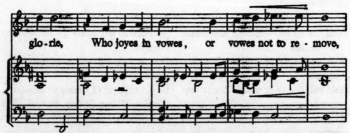

glo - rie, Who joyes in vowes, or vowes not to re - move,

1) Dowland's "FIRST BOOKE" went through four editions during his lifetime. We base our edition of the musical text on the last of these which was printed in 1613.

Who   by   this light-god   hath   not   ben made——

sor - ry: Let   him   see   me   ec

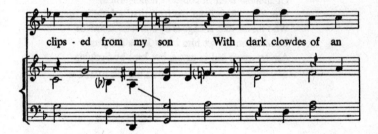

clips - ed   from   my   son   With   dark clowdes   of   an

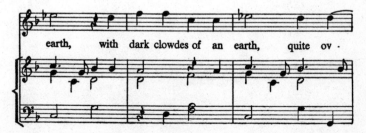

earth,   with   dark clowdes   of   an   earth,   quite   ov ·

er -   runne.   - runne.

1

Who ever thinks or hopes of love for love,
Or who belov'd in *Cupids* lawes doth glorie,
Who joyes in vowes or vowes not to remove,
Who by this light-god hath not ben made sorry:
Let him see me ecclipsed from my son
With dark clowdes of an earth quite overrunne.

2

Who thinks that sorrowes felt, desires hidden,
Or humble faith in constant honor arm'd,
Can keepe love from the fruit that is forbidden,
Who thinks that change is by entreatie charm'd:
Looking on me let him know loves delights
Are treasures hid in caves, but kept by Sprights.

FULKE GREVILLE

IF MY COMPLAINTS

JOHN DOWLAND   THE FIRST BOOKE OF SONGES 1597

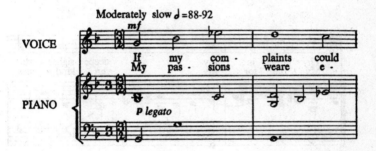

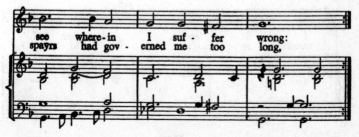

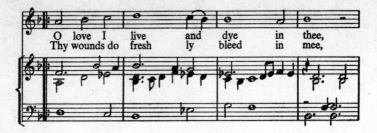

O love I live and dye in thee,
Thy wounds do fresh ly bleed in mee,

Thy griefe in my deepe sighes still
My hart for thy un - kind - nes

speakes, Yet thou dost hope when
breakes, Thou saist thou canst when my

I de - spaire, And when I
harmes re - paire, Yet for re -

84

hope thou makst me hope in vaine.
dresse thou letst me still com· plaine.

1

If my complaints could passions moove,
Or make love see wherein I suffer wrong:
My passions weare enough to proove
That my despayrs had governed me too long.
O love I live and dye in thee,
Thy griefe in my deepe sighes still speakes,
Thy wounds do freshly bleed in mea,
My hart for thy unkindnes breakes,
Yet thou dost hope when I despaire,
And when I hope thou makst me hope in vaine.
Thou saist thou canst my harmes repaire,
Yet for redresse thou letst me still complaine.

2

Can love be ritch and yet I want,
Is love my judge and yet am I condemn'd?
Thou plenty hast, yet me dost scant,
Thou made a god, and yet thy power contemn'd.
That I do live it is thy power,
That I desire it is thy worth,
If love doth make mens lives too soure,
Let me not love, nor live henceforth,
Die shall my hopes, but not my faith
That you that of my fall may hearers be,
May here despaire, which truly saith
I was more true to love than love to me.

ANONYMOUS

CAN SHEE EXCUSE MY WRONGS

JOHN DOWLAND   THE FIRST BOOKE OF SONGES 1597

Moderately fast ♩ = 108-112

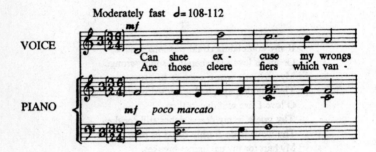

VOICE

Can shee ex - cuse my wrongs
Are those cleere fiers which van -

PIANO

mf poco marcato

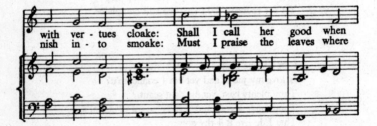

with ver - tues cloake: Shall I call her good when
nish in - to smoake: Must I praise the leaves where

she proves un - kind. No no where
no fruit I find. Cold love is

86

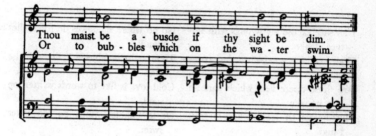

shad - owes do for bod - ies stand,
like to words writ - ten on sand,

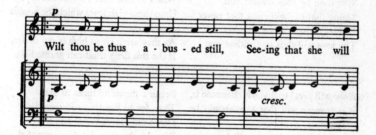

Thou maist be a - busde if thy sight be dim.
Or to bub - bles which on the wa - ter swim.

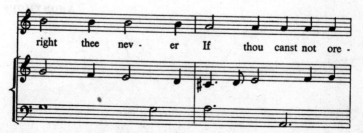

Wilt thou be thus a - bus - ed still, See - ing that she will

right thee nev - er If thou canst not ore -

87

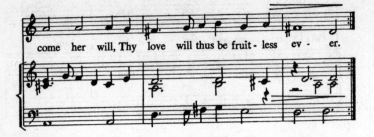

come her will, Thy love will thus be fruit - less ev - er.

1

Can shee excuse my wrongs with ver-
  tues cloake:
Shall I call her good when she proves
  unkind.
Are those cleere fiers which vannish
  into smoake:
Must I praise the leaves where no fruit
  I find.

2

No no where shadowes do for bodies
  stand,
Thou maist be abusde if thy sight be
  dim.
Cold love is like to words written on
  sand,
Or to bubbles which on the water
  swim.

3

Wilt thou be thus abused still,
Seeing that she will right thee never
If thou canst not orecome her will,
Thy love will thus be fruitless ever.

4

Was I so base that I might not aspire
Unto those high joyes which she houlds
  from me,
As they are high so high is my desire,
If she this deny what can granted be.

5

If she will yeeld to that which reason is,
It is reasons will that love should be
  just,
Deare make me happie still by grant-
  ing this,
Or cut off delayes if that dye I must.

6

Better a thousand times to dye
Than for to live thus tormented,
Deare but remember it was I
Who for thy sake did dye contented.

ANONYMOUS

DEARE, IF YOU CHANGE

JOHN DOWLAND   THE FIRST BOOKE OF SONGES 1597

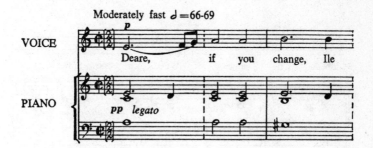

Deare, if you change, Ile

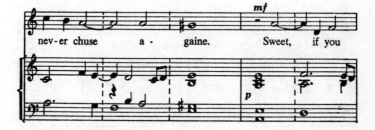

nev-er chuse a-gaine. Sweet, if you

shrinke, Ile nev-er thinke of love.

89

Faire, if you faile, Ile judge all

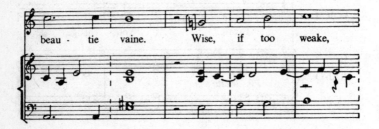

beau - tie vaine. Wise, if too weake,

moe wits Ile nev er prove.

Deare, sweet, faire, wise, change,

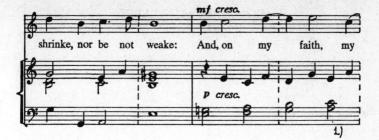

shrinke, nor be not weake: And, on my faith, my

faith shal nev - er breake. breake.

1) original: A♯

1

Deare, if you change, Ile never chuse againe.
Sweet, if you shrink, Ile never thinke of love.
Faire, if you faile, Ile judge all beautie vaine.
Wise, if too weake, moe wits Ile never prove.
   Deare, sweet, faire, wise, change, shrinke, nor be not weake:
   And, on my faith, my faith shal never breake.

2

Earth with her flowers shall sooner heaven adorne,
Heaven her bright stars through earths dim globe shal move,
Fire heate shall loose, and frosts of flame be borne,
Aire made to shine as blacke as hell shall prove:
   Earth, heaven, fire, aire, the world transform'd shall view,
   Ere I prove false to faith, or strange to you.

ANONYMOUS

GO CHRISTALL TEARES

JOHN DOWLAND   THE FIRST BOOKE OF SONGES 1597

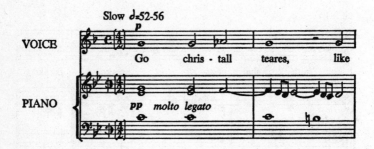

Go chris - tall teares, like

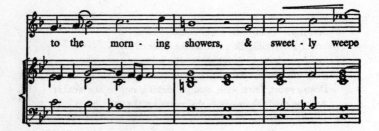

to the morn - ing showers, & sweet - ly weepe

in - to thy La - dies brest,

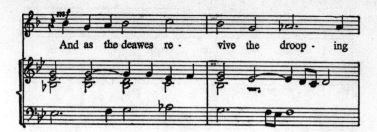

And as the deawes re - vive the droop - ing

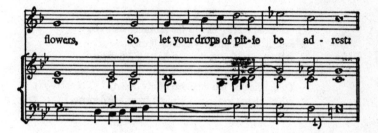

flowers, So let your drops of pit-ie be ad - rest:

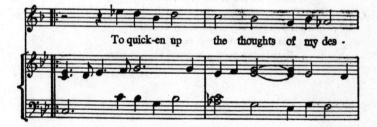

To quick-en up the thoughts of my des -

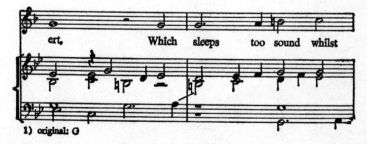

ert, Which sleeps too sound whilst

1) original: G

I   from   her   de-   parte   parte

1

Go christall teares, like to the morning showers,
& sweetly weepe into thy Ladies brest,
And as the deawes revive the dropping flowers,
So let your drops of pitie be adrest:
    To quicken up the thoughts of my desert,
    Which sleeps too sound whilst I from her departe.

2

Haste haplesse sighs and let your burning breath
Dissolve the Ice of her indurate harte,
Whose frosen rigor like forgetfull death,
Feeles never any touch of my desarte:
    Yet sighs and teares to her I sacryfise,
    Both from a spotles hart and pacient eyes.

ANONYMOUS

HIS GOLDEN LOCKS TIME HATH TO SILVER TURNDE

JOHN DOWLAND   THE FIRST BOOKE OF SONGES 1597

His gold - en locks time hath to

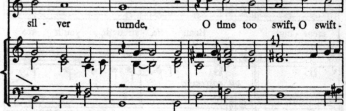

sil - ver turnde,   O time too swift, O swift -

ness nev - er ceas - ing, His youth gainst

1) original: B

time & age hath ev - er spurnde,

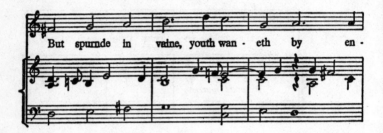

But spurnde in vaine, youth wan - eth by en -

creas - ing: Beau - tie, strength, youth are

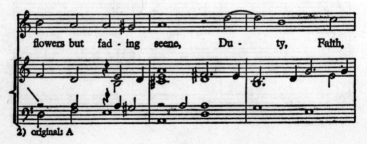

flowers but fad - ing seene, Du - ty, Faith,

2) original: A

96

Love   are roots   and   ev - er greene.

1

His golden locks time hath to silver turnde,
O time too swift, O swiftness never ceasing,
His youth gainst time & age hath ever spurnde,
But spurnde in vaine, youth waneth by encreasing:
   Beautie, strength, youth are flowers but fading seene,
   Duty, Faith, Love are roots and ever greene.

2

His helmet now shall make a hive for bees,
And lovers sonets turne to holy psalmes:
A man at armes must now serve on his knees,
And feed on prayers which are ages almes,
   But though from court to cotage he departe
   His saint is sure of his unspotted hart.

3

And when he saddest sits in homely Cell,
Hele teach his swaines this Caroll for a songe,
Blest be the harts that wish my soveraigne well,
Curst be the soule that thinke her any wrong:
   Goddes allow this aged man his right,
   To be your beadsman now that was your knight.

GEORGE PEELE

COME AWAY, COME SWEET LOVE

JOHN DOWLAND   THE FIRST BOOKE OF SONGES 1597

le lips to kisse, And mixe our
ing Love long pain, Pro - cured by

soules in mutuall blisse.
beau - ties rude dis - daine.

2
Come awaie, come sweet love,
The goulden morning wasts,
While the son from his sphere,
His fierie arrows casts:
Making all the shadowes flie,
Playing, staying in the grove,
To entertaine the stealth of love,
Thither sweet love let us lie,
Flying, dying, in desire,
Wing'd with sweet hopes and heav'nly fire.

3
Come away, come sweet love,
Doe not in vaine adorne
Beauties grace that should rise
Like to the naked morne
Lillies on the rivers side,
And faire Cyprian flowers new blowne,
Desire no beauties but their owne,
Ornament is nurce of pride,
Pleasure, measure, loves delight,
Haste then sweet love our wished flight.

ANONYMOUS

AWAY WITH THESE SELFE LOVING LADS

JOHN DOWLAND THE FIRST BOOKE OF SONGES 1597

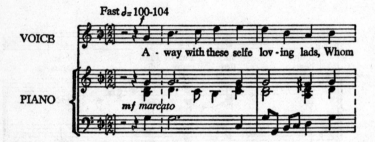

A - way with these selfe lov -ing lads, Whom

Cu - pids ar - rowe nev - er glads: A - way poore soules that

sigh & weepe In love of them that lie & sleepe,

1) original: F♮

For Cu - pid is a med - ooe god, &

foro - eth none to kisse the rod.

2

God *Cupids* shaft like destinie,
Doth either good or ill decree,
Desert is borne out of his bow,
Reward upon his feet doth go,
    What fooles are they that have not
       knowne
    That love likes no lawes but his
       owne?

3

My songs they be of *Cynthias* praise,
I weare her rings on hollidaies,
On every tree I write her name,
And every day I reade the same:
    Where honor, *Cupids* rivall is,
    There miracles are seene of his.

4

If *Cinthia* crave her ring of me,
I blot her name out of the tree,
If doubt do darken things held deere,
Then well fare nothing once a yeere:
    For many run, but one must win,
    Fooles only hedge the Cuckoo in.

5

The worth that worthinesse should
    move
Is love, which is the bowe of love,
And love as well the foster can,
As can the mighty Noble-man:
    Sweet Saint, tis true you worthie be,
    Yet without love nought worth to
      me.

FULKE GREVILLE

COME HEAVY SLEEPE

JOHN DOWLAND   THE FIRST BOOKE OF SONGES 1597

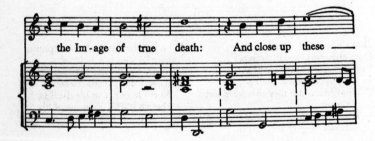

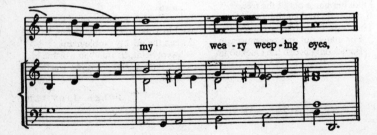

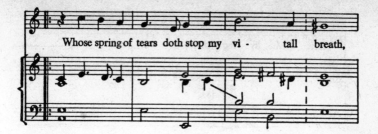

Whose spring of tears doth stop my vi - tall breath,

And tears my hart with sor - rows high swoln crys:

Come & pos - ses my tir - ed thoughts-worne —— soule,

That liv - ing dies, That liv - ing

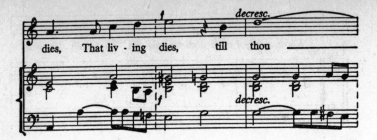

dies, That liv - ing dies, till thou —————

———— on me be stoule.

1

Come heavy sleepe, the Image of true death:
And close up these my weary weeping eyes,
Whose spring of tears doth stop my vitall breath,
And tears my hart with sorrows high swoln crys:
Come & posses my tired thoughts-worne soule,
That living dies, till thou on me be stoule.

2

Come shadow of my end: and shape of rest,*
Alied to death, child to this black fac't night,
Come thou and charme these rebels in my brest,
Whose waking fancies doth my mind affright.
O come sweet sleepe, come or I die for ever,
Come ere my last sleepe coms, or come never.

ANONYMOUS

* To make the words conform naturally to the notes, the singer should follow **Dr.**
Fellowes' suggestion and sing: *Come shape of rest: and shadow of my end.*

THE SECOND BOOKE OF
SONGS OR AYRES 1600

JOHN DOWLAND

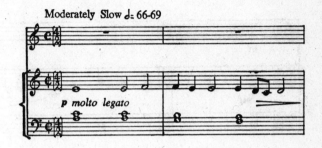

[1] Dowland dedicated this song to Anthony Holborne, an Elizabethan composer widely known for his instrumental music

proud to be ad - vanc - ed

so

mf

p

In those faire eies, in those faire

eies, where all per - fec ——— tions keepe,

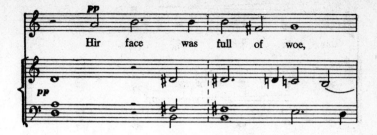

Hir face was full of woe,

full of woe, But such a

woe (be - leeve me) as wins more hearts,

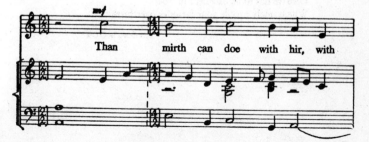

Than mirth can doe with hir, with

hir in · tys · ing parts.

1

I saw my Lady weepe,
And sorrow proud to be advanced so
In those faire eies, where all perfections keepe,
Hir face was full of woe,
But such a woe (beleeve me) as wins more hearts,
Than mirth can doe with hir intysing parts.

2

Sorrow was there made faire,
And passion wise, teares a delightfull thing,
Silence beyond all speech a wisdome rare,
Shee made hir sighes to sing,
And all things with so sweet a sadnesse move,
As made my heart at once both grieve and love.

3

O fayrer than ought ells
The world can shew, leave off in time to grieve,
Inough, inough, your joyfull lookes excells,
Teares kills the heart, believe,
O strive not to be excellent in woe,
Which onely breeds your beauties overthrow.

ANONYMOUS

FLOW MY TEARES
(LACRIME)

JOHN DOWLAND

THE SECOND BOOKE OF
SONGS OR AYRES 1600

nights black bird hir sad in - fa - my
in dis - paire their lost for - tuns de -

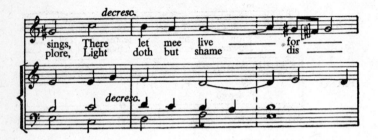

sings, There let mee live for -
plore, Light doth but shame dis

lorne. Nev - er
close. From the

[Somewhat faster]

may my woes be re - liev - ed,
high - est spire of con - tent - ment,

110

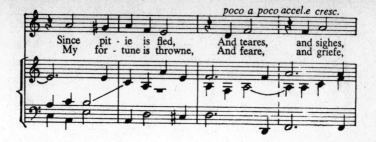

poco a poco accel. e cresc.

Since pit - ie is fled, And teares, and sighes,
My for - tune is throwne, And feare, and griefe,

and grones my wea - rie dayes, my wea - rie dayes,
and paine for my de - serts, for my de - serts,

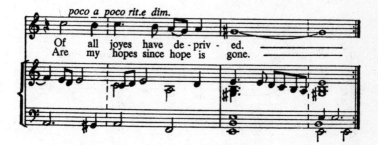

poco a poco rit. e dim.

Of all joyes have de - priv - ed.
Are my hopes since hope is gone.

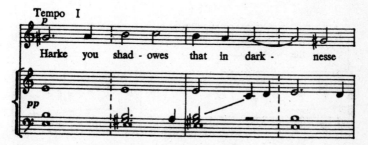

Tempo I

Harke you shad - owes that in dark - nesse

111

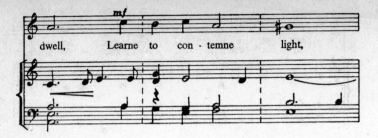

dwell, Learne to con-temne light,

Hap- pie, hap-

pie they that in hell Feele

not the worlds —— de - spite. ——

1

Flow my teares fall from your springs,
Exilde for ever, let me mourne
Where nights black bird hir sad infamy sings,
There let mee live forlorne.

2

Downe vaine lights shine you no more,
No nights are dark enough for those
That in dispaire their lost fortuns deplore,
Light doth but shame disclose.

3

Never may my woes be relieved,
Since pitie is fled,
And teares, and sighes, and grones my wearie dayes
Of all joyes have deprived.

4

From the highest spire of contentment,
My fortune is throwne,
And feare, and griefe, and paine for my deserts,
Are my hopes since hope is gone.

5

Harke you shadowes that in darknesse dwell,
Learne to contemne light,
Happie, happie they that in hell
Feele not the worlds despite.

ANONYMOUS

113

FINE KNACKS FOR LADIES

JOHN DOWLAND

THE SECOND BOOKE OF
SONGS OR AYRES 1600

Fine knacks for la - dies,

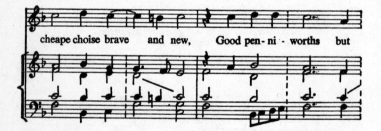

cheape choise brave and new, Good pen - ni - worths but

mon - y can - not move, I keep a

faier but for the faier to view,

A beg - gar may bee li - ber - all of love,

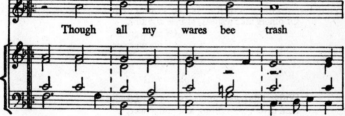

Though all my wares bee trash

the hart is true, The hart is

115

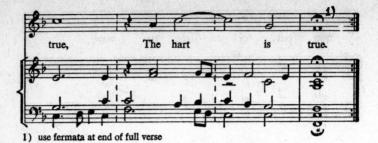

true,   The   hart   is   true.

1) use fermata at end of full verse

1

Fine knacks for ladies, cheape choise brave and new,
Good penniworths but mony cannot move,
I keep a faier but for the faier to view,
A beggar may bee liberall of love,
Though all my wares bee trash the hart is true,
             The hart is true,
             The hart is true.

2

Great gifts are guiles and looke for gifts againe,
My trifles come, as treasures from my minde,
It is a precious Jewell to bee plaine,
Sometimes in shell th' orients pearles we finde,
Of others take a sheaf, of mee a graine,
             Of me a graine,
             Of me a graine.

3

Within this packe pinnes points laces & gloves,
And divers toies fitting a country faier,
But in my hart where duety serves and loves,
Turtels & twins, courts brood, a heavenly paier:
Happy the hart that thincks of no removes,
             Of no removes,
             Of no removes.

                                    ANONYMOUS

O SWEET WOODS

JOHN DOWLAND

THE SECOND BOOKE OF
SONGS OR AYRES 1600

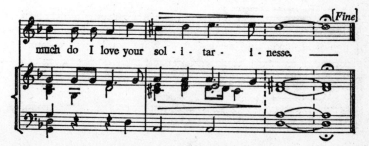

From fames de - sire, from loves de- light re - tir'd,

In these sad groves an Her - mits life I

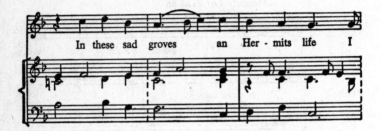

led, And those false pleas - ures

which I once ad - mir'd, With sad re - mem-

brance of my fall, my fall, I dread, To

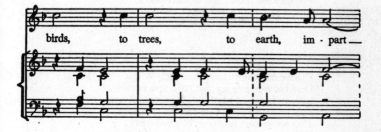

birds, to trees, to earth, im - part ___

___ I this, For shee less

[Da Capo al Fine]

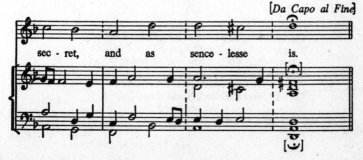

sec - ret, and as sence - lesse is.

119

1

O sweet woods the delight of solitarinesse,
O how much do I love your solitarinesse.

From fames desire, from loves delight retir'd,
In these sad groves an Hermits life I led,
And those false pleasures which I once admir'd,
With sad remembrance of my fall, I dread,
To birds, to trees, to earth, impart I this,
For shee less secret, and as sencelesse is.
                    O sweet woods, &c.
                    O how much, &c.

2

Experience which repentance onely brings,
Doth bid mee now my hart from love estrange,
Love is disdained when it doth looke at Kings,
And love loe placed, base and apt to change:
Ther power doth take from him his liberty,
Hir want of worth makes him in cradell die.
                    O sweet woods, &c.
                    O how much, &c.

3

You men that give false worship unto Love,
And seeke that which you never shall obtaine,
The endlesse worke of Sisiphus you procure,
Whose end is this, to know you strive in vaine,
Hope and desire which now your Idols bee,
You needs must loose and feele dispaire with mee.
                    O sweet woods, &c.
                    O how much, &c.

4

You woods in you the fairest Nimphs have walked,
Nimphs at whose sight all harts did yeeld to Love.
You woods in whom deere lovers oft have talked,
How doe you now a place of mourning prove,
Wansted my Mistres saith this is the doome,
Thou art loves Childbed, Nursery, and Tombe.
                    O sweet woods, &c.
                    O how much, &c.

SIR PHILIP SIDNEY

IN DARKNESSE LET MEE DWELL

JOHN DOWLAND

A MUSICAL BANQUET 1610

1) original ♪

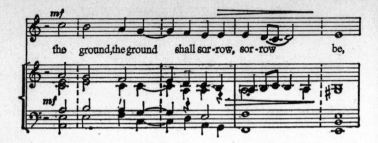

the ground, the ground   shall sor-row, sor-row   be,

The roofe Di - spaire   to barre all,

all cheer-ful_____ light   from mee,

The   wals   of   mar -   ble

blacke that _____ moist - ned, that

moist - ned still shall

weepe, _____ still shall weepe,

My mu - sicke, My mu -

sicke hell - ish, hell - ish

jar - ring _____ sounds, jar - ring, jar-ring sounds to ___

decresc.

_____ ban - ish, ban - ish friend - ly sleepe. _____

decresc.

p

Thus wed - ded

p

1) original: B   2) original: F♯ below B

124

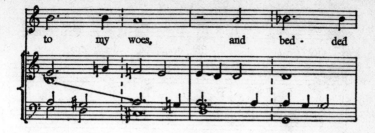

to   my   woes,   and   bed - ded

to   my   Tombe, _____

O _____   let me   liv - ing die,

marcato

O   let me liv - ing, let me liv -   ing, liv - ing

125

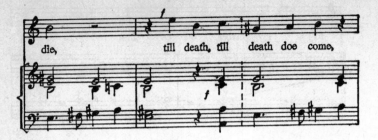

die,   till death, till   death doe come,

till death, till   death doe come, till   death, ———

— till ——— death doe come.

In ——— dark -   nesse ——

let ——— me ——————— dwell.

In darknesse let mee dwell, the ground shall sorrow be,
The roofe Dispaire to barre all cheerful light from mee,
The wals of marble blacke that moistned still shall weepe,
My musicke hellish jarring sounds to banish friendly sleepe.
Thus wedded to my woes, and bedded to my Tombe,
O let me living die, till death doe come.

ANONYMOUS

WEEPE YOU NO MORE

THE THIRD AND LAST BOOKE OF
SONGS OR AIRES 1603

JOHN DOWLAND

Weepe ———— you no more sad

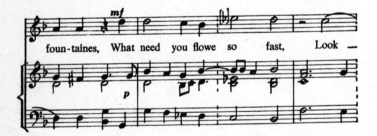

foun-taines, What need you flowe so fast, Look ——

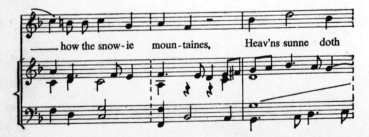

—— how the snow-ie moun-taines, Heav'ns sunne doth

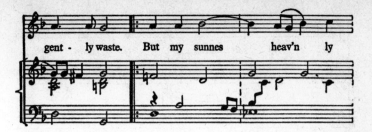

gent - ly waste. But my sunnes heav'n ly

eyes View not your weep - ing,

That _____ nowe lie sleep -

- ing, that _____ nowe lie sleep - ing, Soft _____

1) original: barline here

129

1

Weepe you no more sad fountaines,
    What need you flowe so fast,
Look how the snowie mountaines,
    Heav'ns sunne doth gently waste.
But my sunnes heav'nly eyes
    View not your weeping,
    That nowe lies sleeping
Softly, now softly lies
    Sleeping.

2

Sleepe is a reconciling,
    A rest that peace begets:
Doth not the sunne rise smiling,
    When faire at ev'n he sets,
Rest you, then rest sad eyes,
    Melt not in weeping,
    While she lies sleeping
Softy, now softly lies
    Sleeping.

ANONYMOUS

THE LOWEST TREES HAVE TOPS

JOHN DOWLAND

THE THIRD AND LAST BOOKE OF
SONGS OR AIRES 1603

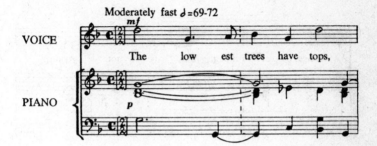

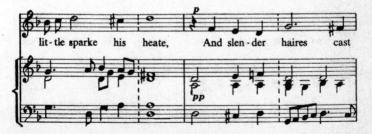

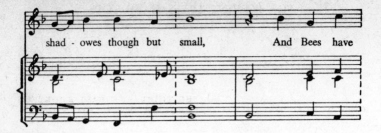

shad - owes though but small, And Bees have

stings al - though they be not great.

Seas have their source, and

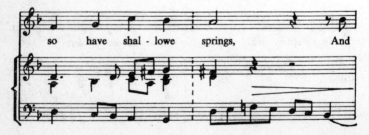

so have shal - lowe springs, And

love   is love   in beg - gars and   in   kings.

1

The lowest trees have tops, the Ant her gall,
The flie her spleene, the little sparke his heate,
And slender haires cast shadowes though but small,
And Bees have stings although they be not great.
Seas have their source, and so have shallowe springs,
And love is love in beggars and in kings.

2

Where waters smoothest run, deep are the foords,
The diall stirres, yet none perceives it move:
The firmest faith is in the fewest words,
The Turtles cannot sing, and yet they love,
True hearts have eyes and eares, no tongues to speake:
They heare, and see, and sigh, and then they breake.

ATTRIBUTED TO SIR EDWARD DYER

COME MY CELIA

ALFONSO FERRABOSCO

AYRES 1609

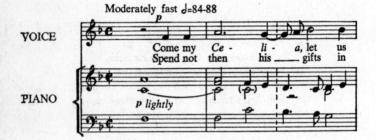

Come my Ce - li - a, let us
Spend not then his ___ gifts in

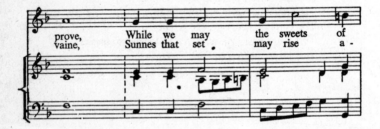

prove, While we may the sweets of
vaine, Sunnes that set . may rise a -

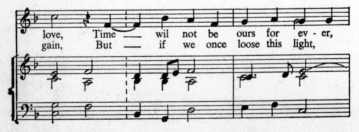

love, Time ___ wil not be ours for ev - er,
gain, But ___ if we once loose this light,

He at length our good ——————— will sev - er,
Tis with us per-pet - ——————— u - all night.

Why should wee de - ferre our joyes? Fame and

ru - mour are but toyes. Can - not we ——— de - lude the

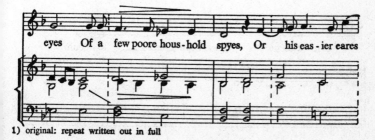

eyes Of a few poore hous - hold spyes, Or his eas - ier eares

1) original: repeat written out in full

135

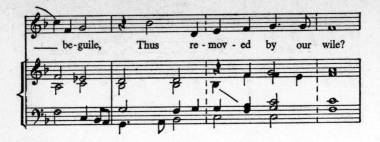

be - guile, Thus re - mov - ed by our wile?

'Tis no sinne loves fruits to steale, But the sweet

theft to re - veale, To be tak - en,

to be seene, These have crimes _____ ac - count - ed

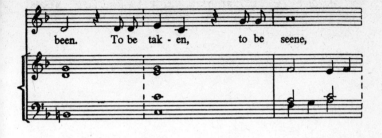

been. To be tak - en, to be seene,

These have crimes ———— ac - count — ed been.

Come my *Celia*, let us prove,
While we may the sweets of love,
Time wil not be ours for ever,
He at length our good will sever,
Spend not then his gifts in vaine,
Sunnes that set may rise again,
But if we once loose this light,
Tis with us perpetuall night.
Why should wee deferre our joyes?
Fame and rumour are but toyes.
Cannot we delude the eyes
Of a few poore houshold spyes,
Or his easier eares beguile,
Thus removed by our wile?
'Tis no sinne loves fruits to steale,
But the sweet theft to reveale,
To be taken, to be seene,
These have crimes accounted been.

BEN JONSON

ALFONSO FERRABOSCO

AYRES 1609

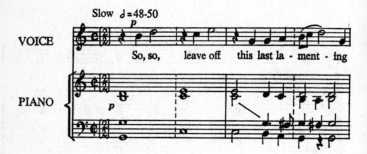

So, so, leave off this last la - ment - ing

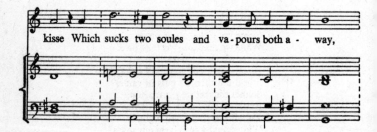

kisse Which sucks two soules and va - pours both a - way,

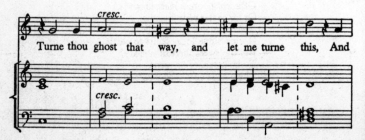

Turne thou ghost that way, and let me turne this, And

let our selves be - night our ———— hap - py

day,   *mf* We aske none leave to

love, nor wil we owe   An - y so cheape

a death ———— as say - ing goe.   *p* We aske none

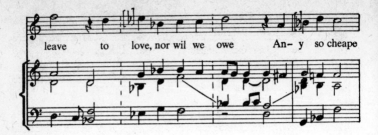

leave   to   love, nor wil we owe   An- y so cheape

a death _____ as say - ing goe.

1

So, so, leave off this last lamenting kisse
Which sucks two soules and vapours both away,
Turne thou ghost that way, and let me turne this,
And let our selves benight our happy day,
    We aske none leave to love, nor wil we owe
    Any so cheape a death as saying goe.

2

Goe, goe, and if that word have not quite kild thee,
Ease me with death by bidding me goe too.
O, if it have let my word worke on me,
And a just office on a murderer doe.
    Except it be too late to kill me so,
    Being double dead, going and bidding goe.

JOHN DONNE: THE EXPIRATION

SO BEAUTIE ON THE WATERS STOOD

ALFONSO FERRABOSCO

AYRES 1609

So _____ beau - tie on the wa - ters

stood, When _____ Love had sev - er'd earth from floud,

So _____ when he part - ed ayre from

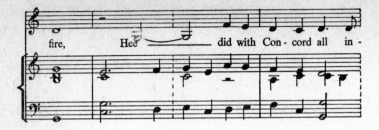

fire, Hee _____ did with Con - cord all in -

spire, And _____ then a mo - tion _____

_____ hee them taught, That _____ eld - er

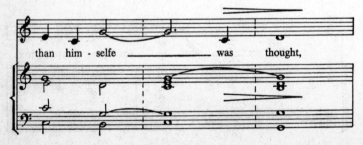

than him - selfe _____ was thought,

Which thought was yet the childe of earth, For love is eld - er than his birth. birth.

So beautie on the waters stood,
When Love had sever'd earth from floud,
So when he parted ayre from fire,
Hee did with Concord all inspire,
And then a motion hee them taught,
That elder than himselfe was thought,
Which thought was yet the childe of earth.
For love is elder than his birth.

BEN JONSON

WHAT THEN IS LOVE

THOMAS FORD

MUSICKE OF SUNDRIE KINDES 1607

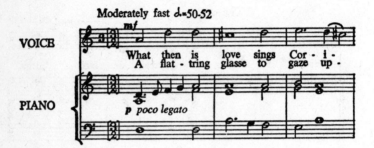

VOICE

What then is love sings Cor - i -
A flat - tring glasse to gaze up-

PIANO

p poco legato

don Since Phil - li - da is growne so coy.
on, A bus - ie jest, a se - rious toy.

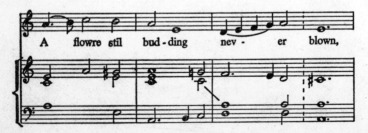

A flowre stil bud - ding nev - er blown,

144

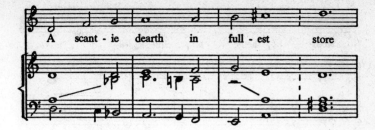

A scant-ie dearth in full-est store

Yeeld-ing least fruite where most is sowne,

My dal-ie note shal be there-fore,

Heigh ho heigh ho chill love no more,

1)

1) original has barline here

Heigh   ho, heigh   ho,   chill   love   no   more.

1

What then is love sings Coridon
Since Phillida is growne so coy.
A flattring glasse to gaze upon,
A busie jest, a serious toy.
A flowre stil budding never blown,
A scantie dearth in fullest store
Yeelding least fruite where most is sowne,
  My dalie note shall be therefore,
      Heigh ho heigh ho chill* love no more,
      Heigh ho heigh ho chill love no more.

2

Tis like a morning dewie rose
Spread fairely to the suns arise,
But when his beames he doth disclose,
That which then flourisht quickly dies,
It is a selfe fed dying hope,
A promisde blisse, a salveless sore,
An aimelesse marke, an erring scope,
  My dailie note shall be therefore,
      Heigh ho, &c.

3

Tis like a Lampe shining to all,
Whilst in it selfe it doth decay,
It seemes to free, whome it doth thrall,
And leades our pathles thoughts astray,
It is the spring of wintred harts,
Parcht by the summers heate before,
Faint hope to kindly warmth converts,
  My daily note shall be therefore,
      Heigh ho, &c.

ANONYMOUS

*chill: I'll

146

SINCE FIRST I SAW YOUR FACE

THOMAS FORD   MUSICKE OF SUNDRIE KINDES 1607

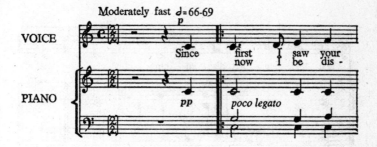

Since first I saw your
now I be dis-

face I re-solvde to hon-our & re-nowne yee, If
dayn-ed I wishe my hart had nev-er

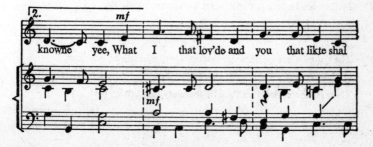

knowne yee, What I that lov'de and you that likte shal

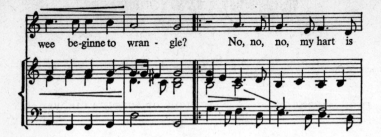

wee be-ginne to wran - gle? No, no, no, my hart is

fast and can - not dis - en - tan - gle. gle.

1

Since first I saw your face I resolvde to honour & renowne yee,
If now I be disdayned I wishe my hart had never knowne yee,
What I that lov'de and you that likte shal wee beginne to wrangle?
No, no, no, my hart is fast and cannot disentangle.

2

If I admire or prayse you too much, that fault you may forgive mee,
Or if my hands had stray'd but a touch, then justly might you leave mee,
I askt you leave, you bad me love, ist now a time to chide me?
No, no, no, Ile love you still, what fortune ere betide me.

8

The Sunne whose beames most glorious are, rejecteth no beholder,
And your sweet beautie past compare, made my poore eyes the boulder,
Where beautie moves, and wit delights, and signes of kindnes bind me
There, O there where ere I go, Ile leave my hart behind me.

ANONYMOUS

THERE IS A LADIE SWEET AND KIND

THOMAS FORD   MUSICKE OF SUNDRIE KINDES 1607

There is a La-die sweet & kind,

Was nev - er face so pleasde my mind,

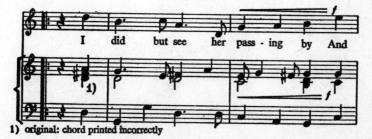

I did but see her pass - ing by And

1) original: chord printed incorrectly

149

yet   I love   her   till   I   die.

1) original: F

1

There is a Ladie sweet & kind,
Was never face so pleasde my mind,
I did but see her passing by
And yet I love her till I die.

2

Her jesture, motion and her smiles,
Her wit, her voyce, my hart beguiles,
Beguiles my hart, I know not why,
And yet I love her till I die.

3

Her free behaviour winning lookes,
Will make a Lawyer burne his bookes,
I toucht her not, alas not I,
And yet I love her till I die.

4

Had I her fast betwixt mine armes,
Judge you that thinke such sports were
    harmes,
Wert any harm? no, no, fie, fie,
For I will love her till I die.

5

Should I remaine confined there,
So long as Phebus in his spher,
I to request, shee to denie,
Yet would I love her till I die.

6

Cupid is winged and doth range,
Her countrie so my love doth change,
But change the earth, or change the
    skie,
Yet will I love her till I die.

ANONYMOUS

WHAT IS BEAUTY BUT A BREATH

THOMAS GREAVES   SONGS OF SUNDRIE KINDES 1604

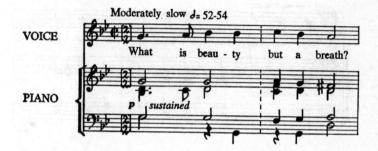

VOICE

What is beau-ty but a breath?

PIANO

p *sustained*

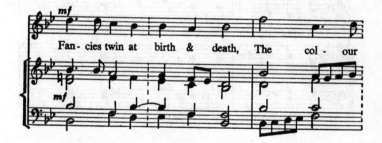

mf

Fan - cies twin at birth & death, The col - our

mf

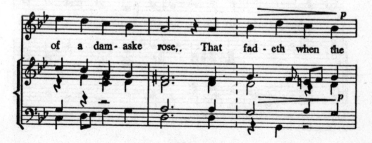

of a dam - aske rose,. That fad - eth when the

p

p

north-wind blowes: Tis such that though all sorts do

crave it, They know not what it is to have it: —

A thing that som time stoops not to a king

And yet most o-pen to the com-monst thing: For she

1) original: incorrect rhythmic values
2) original: F

that is most fair, Is o - pen

to the aire.

1

What is beauty but a breath?
Fancies twin at birth & death,
The colour of a damaske rose,
That fadeth when the northwind blowes:
Tis such that though all sorts do crave it,
They know not what it is to have it:
A thing that som time stoops not to a king
And yet most open to the commonst thing:
For she that is most fair,
Is open to the aire.

ANONYMOUS

TOBACCO IS LIKE LOVE

TOBIAS HUMB

MUSICALL HUMORS 1605

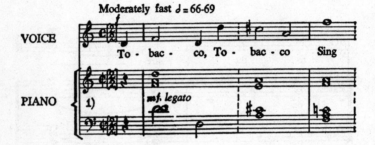

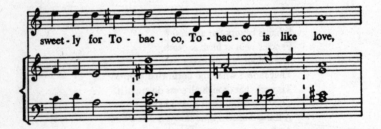

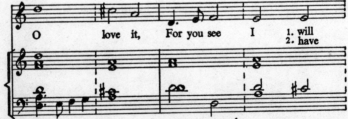

1) original Lute part a fifth lower, voice part untransposed.

prove it. Love mak - eth leane the
provde it.

fatte mens tu - mor, So doth To - bac - co,

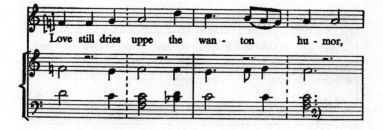

Love still dries uppe the wan - ton hu - mor,

So doth To - bac - co, Love makes men sayle from shore to

1) original: whole tone higher
2) original: semitone lower

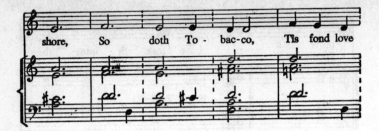

shore, So doth To - bac-co, Tis fond love

of - ten makes men poor, So doth To -

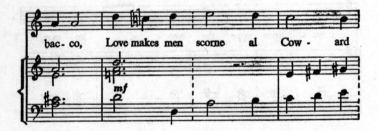

bac-co, Love makes men scorne al Cow - ard

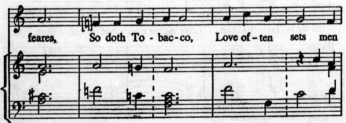

feares, So doth To - bac-co, Love of - ten sets men

original: whole tone lower.

by   the   eares,   So   doth   To - bac - co.

1

Tobacco, Tobacco
Sing sweetly for Tobacco,
Tobacco is like love,
    O love it,
For you see I will prove it.

2

Love makefh leane the fatte mens tumor,
    So doth Tobacco,
Love still dries uppe the wanton humor,
    So doth Tobacco,
Love makes men sayle from shore to shore,
    So doth Tobacco,
Tis fond love often makes men poor,
    So doth Tobacco,
Love màkes men scorne al Coward feares,
    So doth Tobacco,
Love often 'sets men by the eares,
    So doth Tobacco.

3

Tobaccoe, Tobaccoe
Sing sweetly for Tobaccoe,
Tobaccoe is like Love,
    O love it,
For you see I have provde it.

                              ANONYMOUS

FAIN WOULD I CHANGE THAT NOTE

TOBIAS HUME

MUSICALL HUMORS 1605

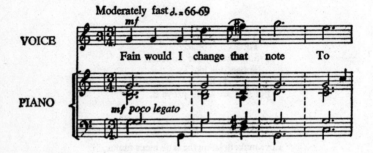

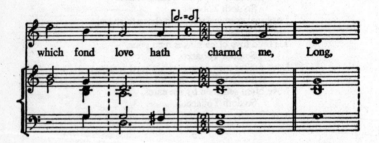

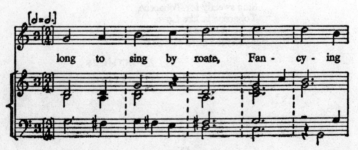

that that harmde me, Yet when this thought doth

1)

come _____ Love is the per - fect

summe Of all de - light:

I have no oth - er choice Ei - ther for

1) original 𝅗𝅥.

pen   or   voyse,   To   sing   or   write.

1) original 𝅘𝅥 𝅘𝅥

1

Fain would I change that note
To which fond love hath charmd me,
Long, long to sing by roate,
Fancying that that harmde me,
   Yet when this thought doth come
   Love is the perfect summe
      Of all delight:
   I have no other choice
   Either for pen or voyse,
       To sing or write.

2

O Love they wrong thee much
That say thy sweete is bitter,
When thy ripe fruit is such,
As nothing can be sweeter,
   Faire house of joy and blisse,
   Where truest pleasure is,
      I do adore thee:
   I know thee what thou art,
   I serve thee with my hart,
      And fall before thee.

ANONYMOUS

WHEN LOVE ON TIME AND MEASURE
MAKES HIS GROUND

ROBERT JONES   THE FIRST BOOKE OF SONGS & AYRES 1600

When love on time and

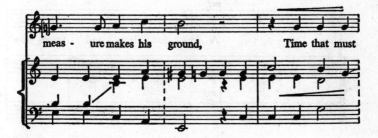

meas - ure makes his ground,   Time that must

end though love —— can nev - er die,   Tis

1) original: barline here

love be-twixt a shad-ow and a sound, A

love not in the hart but in ———— the eie,

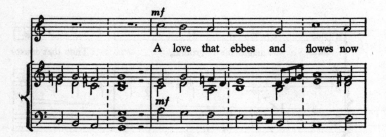

A love that ebbes and flowes now

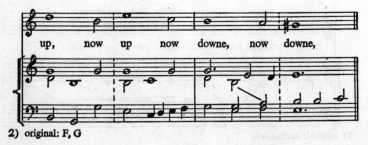

up, now up now downe, now downe,

2) original: F, G

162

A morn-ings fa - vor and an eve - nings frowne. frowne.

1

When love on time and measure makes his ground,
Time that must end though love can never die,
Tis love betwixt a shadow and a sound,
A love not in the hart but in the eie,
   A love that ebbes and flowes now up now downe,
   A mornings favor and an evenings frowne.

2

Sweete lookes shew love, yet they are but as beames,
Faire wordes seeme true, yet they are but as wind,
Eies shed their teares yet are but outward streames:
Sighes paint a sadnes in the falsest minde.
   Lookes, wordes, teares, sighes, shew love when love they leave,
   False harts can weepe, sigh, sweare, and yet deceive.

ATTRIBUTED TO JOHN LILLIATT

DREAMES AND IMAGINATIONS

ROBERT JONES   THE SECOND BOOKE OF SONGS & AYRES 1601

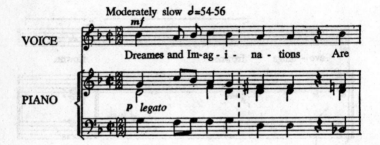

Moderately slow ♩=54-56

VOICE

Dreames and Im-ag - i - na - tions   Are

PIANO

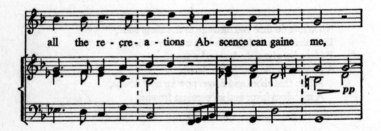

all   the re - cre - a - tions Ab- scence can gaine   me,

Dreames ——— when I wake,   dreames ——

1) original: E♮ in Lute part, E♭ in Bass part

164

when I wake, con - found me, Thoughts for her sake doth wound me Lest she dis - daine me, Then sink - ing let me lie, Or think - ing let me die, Since love,

1)

2) original: F♯ in voice part,
   F♮ in Lute part

165

since   love,   since   love _____

hath slaine   me.   Then   me.

1) original: E♮ in Lute part,
    E♭ in Bass part
2) original: repeat written out in full

1

Dreames and Imaginations
Are all the recreations
  Absence can gaine me,
Dreames when I wake, confound me,
Thoughts for her sake doth wound me
  Lest she disdaine me,
Then sinking let me lie,
Or thinking let me die,
  Since love hath slaine me.

2

Dreames are but coward and doe
Much good they dare not stand to,
  Asham'd of the morrow,
Thoughts like a child that winketh,
Hee's not beguild that thinketh,
  Hath peir'st me thorow,
Both filling me with blisses,
Both killing me with kisses,
  Dying in sorrow.

3

Dreames with their false pretences,
And thoughts confounds my senses
  In the conclusion,
Which like a glasse did shew mee
What came to passe and threw mee
  Into confusion,
Shee made me leave all other,
Yet had she got another,
  This was abusion.

ANONYMOUS

NOW WHAT IS LOVE

ROBERT JONES   THE SECOND BOOKE OF SONGS & AYRES 1601

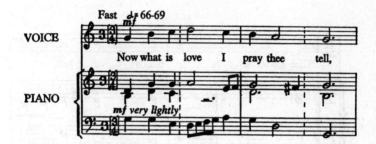

Now what is love I pray thee tell,

It is that foun - taine and that well

Where pleas - ures and re - pent - ance dwell,

1) original: AGB

It is per - haps that sans - ing bell

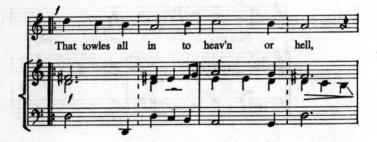

That towles all in to heav'n or hell,

And this is love, and this is

love as I heare tell. tell.

1) original: C♯ in voice part,
   C♮ in Lute part
2) original: repeat written out in full

1

Now what is love I pray thee tell,
It is that fountaine and that well
Where pleasures and repentance dwell,
It is perhaps that sansing bell*
That towles all in to heav'n or hell,
And this is love as I heare tell.

2

Now what is love I praie thee saie,
It is a worke on holy daie,
It is December match't with Maie,
When lustie blood in fresh arraie
Heare ten monethes after of their plaie,
And this is love as I heare saie.

3

Now what is love I praie thee faine,
It is a Sunne-shine mixt with raine,
It is a gentle pleasing paine,
A flower that dyes and springs againe,
It is a noe that wou'd full faine,
And this is love as I heare saine.

4

Yet what is love I praie thee saie,
It is a pretie shadie waie,
As well found out by night as daie,
It is a thing will soone decaie,
Then take the vantage whilst you maie,
And this is love as I heare saie.

5

Now what is love I praie thee show,
A thing that creepes, it cannot goe,
A prize that passeth to and fro,
A thing for one, a thing for moe,
And he that proves shall find it so,
And this is love as I well know.

sansing bell: sanctus bell

ATTRIBUTED TO SIR WALTER RALEIGH

BEAUTY SATE BATHING

ROBERT JONES

ULTIMUM VALE, OR
THE THIRD BOOKE OF AYRES 1605

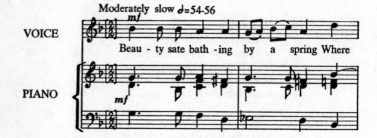

Beau - ty sate bath -ing by a spring Where

fair - est shades did hide her, The windes blew calme, the

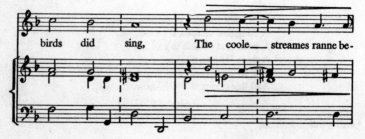

birds did sing, The coole___ streames ranne be-

170

side her, My wan-ton thoughtes in-tiste my eye To see what was for-bid-den, But bet-ter mem-o-ry cride fie, So vaine ___ de-lights were chid-den. My chid-den.

1

Beauty sate bathing by a spring
Where fairest shades did hide her,
The windes blew calme, the birds did
    sing,
The coole streames ranne beside her,
    My wanton thoughtes intiste my
      eye
      To see what was forbidden,
      But better memory cride fie,
      So vaine delights were chidden.

2

Into a slumber then I fell,
But fond imagination
Seemed to see, but could not tell
Her feature or her fashion.
    But even as babes in dreames do
      smile
    And sometime fall aweeping:
    So I awakt as wise the while
    As when I fell asleeping.

ANTHONY MUNDAY

GOE TO BED SWEETE MUZE

ROBERT JONES

ULTIMUM VALE, OR
THE THIRD BOOKE OF AYRES 1605

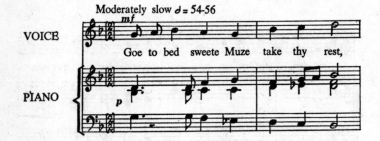

Goe to bed sweete Muze take thy rest,

Let not thy soule bee so op - prest

Though shee de - ny thee, She doth but trie thee,

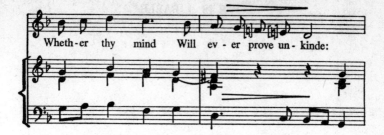

Wheth-er thy mind Will ev-er prove un-kinde:

mf
O love is but a bit-ter— sweete Jest.

1) use fermata at end of full verse

1
Goe to bed sweete Muze take thy rest,
Let not thy soule bee so opprest
 Though shee deny thee,
 She doth but trie thee,
 Whether thy mind
Will ever prove unkinde:
O love is but a bitter-sweete Jest.

2
Muze not upon her smiling lookes,
Thinke that they are but baited hookes,
 Love is a fancy,
 Love is a Franzy,
 Let not a toy
Then breed thee such annoy,
But leave to looke uppon such fond
 bookes.

3
Learne to forget such idle toyes,
Fitter for youthes, and youthfull boyes,
 Let not one sweete smile
 Thy true love beguile,
 Let not a frowne
For ever cast thee downe,
Then sleepe and go to bed in these
 joyes.

ANONYMOUS

173

ROBERT JONES   THE SECOND BOOKE OF SONGS & AYRES 1601

VOICE

Love,   love,   love,   love,

PIANO

mf lightly

love is a ba - ble,   love is a ba - ble,   No

___ man is a - ble   To   say   tis

p legato

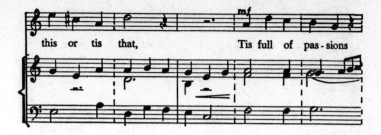

this or tis that, Tis full of pas-sions

Of sun-dry fash-ions, Tis

pp very lightly

like, tis like, tis like I can-not,

cresc.

cresc.

I can-not, I can-not, tis like, _____

mf

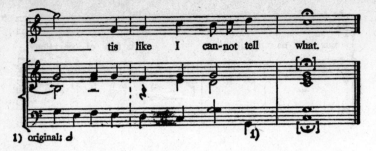

tis like I can-not tell what.

1) original: ♩

1

Love is a bable,
  No man is able
To say tis this or tis that,
  Tis full of passions
  Of sundry fashions,
Tis like I cannot tell what.

2

Loves fayre i'th Cradle,
  Foule in the sable,*
Tis eyther too cold or too hot,
  An arrand lyar,
  Fed by desire,
It is, and yet is not.

3

Love is a fellowe,
  Clad oft m yellowe,
The canker-worme of the mind,
  A privie mischiefe,
  And such a slye thiefe,
No man knowes which waie to find.

4

Love is a woonder,
  That's here and yonder,
As common to one as to moe,
  A monstrous cheater,
  Everie mans debter,
Hang him, and so let him goe.

ANONYMOUS

*the sable: the dark

WHAT IF I SPED

ROBERT JONES

ULTIMUM VALE, OR
THE THIRD BOOKE OF AYRES 1605

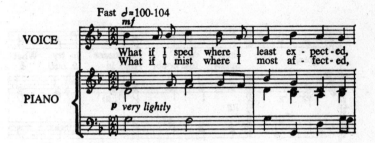

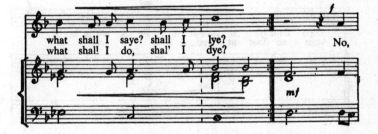

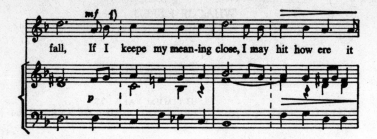

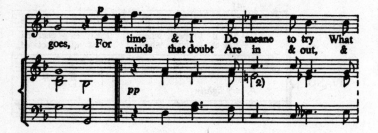

1) original ♩
2) original:

1

What if I sped where I least expected, what shall I saye? shall I lye?
What if I mist where I most affected, what shall I do, shall I dye?
      No, no, Ile have at all,
      Tis as my game doth fall,
      If I keepe my meaning close,
      I may hit how ere it goes,
      For time & I
      Do meane to try
      What hope doth lye in youth, fa la la:
      The minds that doubt
      Are in & out,
      & women flout at truth: fa la la.

2

She whome above the skies I renowned, she whome I loved, shee,
Can she leave all in leathe drowned, can she be coy to me?
      Her passions are but cold,
      She stands and doth beholde,
      She retaines her lookes estrangde,
      As if heaven and earth were changde.
      I speake, she heares,
      I touch, she feares,
      Herein appeares her wit, fa la la:
      I catch, she flies,
      I hold, she cries,
      And still denies, and yet fa la la.

3

May not a wanton looke like a woman, tell me the reason why?
And if a blinde man chance of a birdes nest, must he be pratling? fye:
      What mortall strength can keepe,
      That's got as in a sleepe:
      The felony is his
      That brags of a stoln kis:
      For when we met,
      Both in a net,
      That *Vulcan* set, were hid, fa, la la la:
      And so god wot
      We did it not,
      Or else forgot we did. Fa la la la.

ANONYMOUS

SWEET IF YOU LIKE AND LOVE ME STIL

ROBERT JONES

ULTIMUM VALE, OR
THE THIRD BOOKE OF AYRES 1605

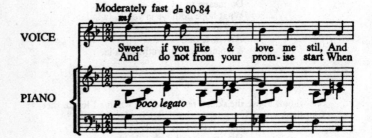

Moderately fast ♩= 80-84

VOICE

Sweet   if you like   &   love me stil, And
And   do not from your   prom-ise start When

PIANO

p poco legato

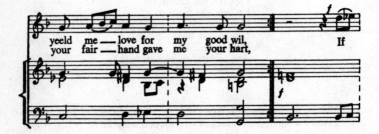

yeeld   me — love for   my   good wil,   If
your   fair — hand gave   me   your hart,

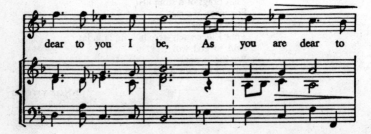

dear   to you   I   be,   As   you   are dear   to

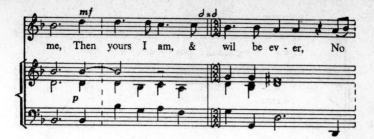

me, Then yours I am, & wil be ev - er, No

time   nor place   my   love   shall   sev - er,

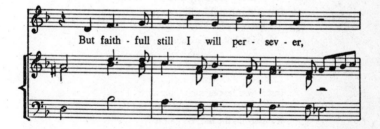

But faith - full still   I   will   per - sev - er,

Like   con - stant Mar - ble   stone,

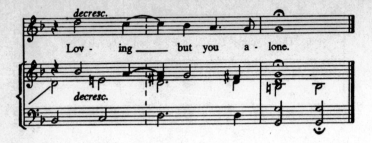

Lov - ing ____ but you a - lone.

1

Sweet if you like & love me stil,
And yeeld me love for my good wil,
And do not from your promise start
When your fair hand gave me your hart,
   If dear to you I be,
   As you are dear to me,
Then yours I am, & wil be ever,
No time nor place my love shall sever,
But faithfull still I will persever,
   Like constant Marble stone,
   Loving but you alone.

2

But if you favour moe than me,*
(Who loves thee still, and none but thee,)
If others do the harvest gaine,
That's due to me for all my paine:
   Yet that you love to range,
   And oft to chop and change.
Then get you some new fangled mate:
My doting love shal turne to hate,
Esteeming you (though too too late)
   Not worth a peble stone,
   Loving not me alone.

FRANCIS DAVISON

*the original has *one*

SWEETE KATE

ROBERT JONES

**A MUSICALL DREAMB
OR THE FOURTH BOOKB OF AYRES 1609**

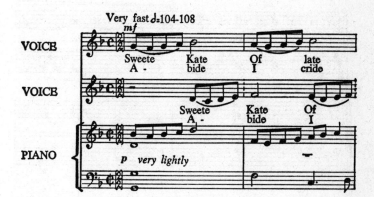

Te hee hee quoth shee   Glad - ly would I

Te hee hee quoth shee   Glad-ly would I see

pp poco marcato

see   An- y man to die   with   lov -

An - y man to die   with   lov -

ing,   Nev- er an-y   yet   Died of such a

ing, Nev-er an-y yet   Died of such a fitte:

184

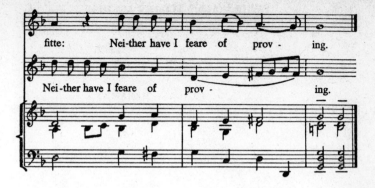

fitte: Nei-ther have I feare of prov- ing.

Nei-ther have I feare of prov- ing.

1

Sweete Kate
Of late
Ran away and left me playning.
Abide
I cride
Or I die with thy disdayning.
Te hee hee quoth shee
Gladly would I see
Any man to die with loving,
Never any yet
Died of such a fitte:
Neither have I feare of proving.

2

Unkind,
I find
Thy delight is in tormenting,
Abide,
I cride,
Or I die with thy consenting.
Te hee hee quoth she,
Make no foole of me,
Men I know have oathes at pleasure,
But their hopes attaind,
They bewray they faind,
And their oathes are kept at leasure.

3

Her words
Like swords
Cut my sorry heart in sunder,
Her floutes,
With doubts,
Kept my heart affections under.
Te hee hee quoth shee,
What a foole is he
Stands in awe of once denying,
Cause I had inough
To become more rough,
So I did, O happy trying.

ANONYMOUS

185

WILL SAIDE TO HIS MAMMY

A MUSICALL DREAME
OR THE FOURTH BOOKE OF AYRES 1609

ROBERT JONES

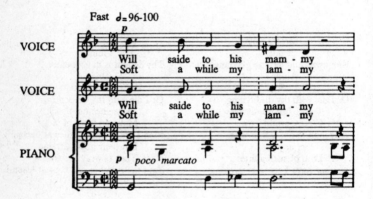

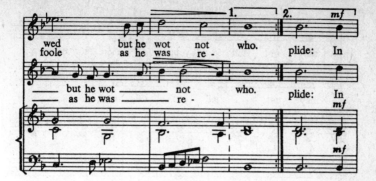

wed   but he wot   not   who.   plide: In
foole   as he was   re -

but he wot   not   who.   plide: In
as he was   re -

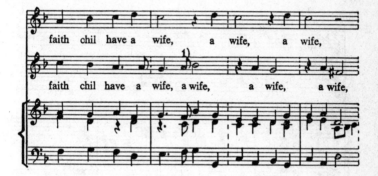

faith chil have a wife,   a wife,   a wife,

faith chil have a wife, a wife,   a wife,   a wife,

O   what a life do I lead For a wife in my bed I

O what a life   do I lead For a wife in my bed   I

1) original: G

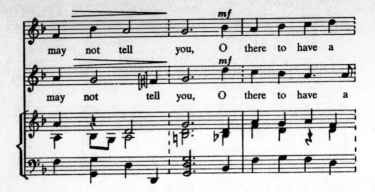

may   not   tell   you,   O   there   to   have   a

may   not   tell   you,   O   there   to   have   a

wife,   a   wife,   a   wife,   O   tis   a

wife,   a   wife,   a   wife,   a   wife,   O   tis   a   smart

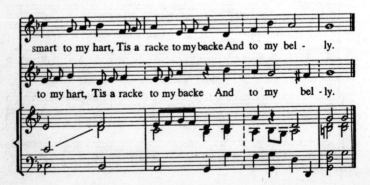

smart   to my hart,   Tis a   racke to my backe And   to   my   bel -   ly.

to my hart,   Tis a   racke   to my backe   And   to   my   bel - ly.

1

Will saide to his mammy
    That hee woulde goe woo,
Faine would he wed but he wot not
    who.
    Soft a while my lammy
Stay, and yet abide.
    Hee like a foole as he was replide:
In faith chil* have a wife, a wife, a
    wife,
    O what a life do I lead
For a wife in my bed
    I may not tell you,
O there to have a wife, a wife, a wife,
    O tis a smart to my hart,
Tis a racke to my backe
    And to my belly.

2

Scarcely was hee wedded,
    Full a fortnights space,
But that he was in a heavie case.
    Largely was he headded,
And his cheekes lookt thinne:
    And to repent he did thus beginne:
A figge for such a wife, a wife, a wife,
    O what a life do I lead,
With a wife in my bedde,
    I may not tell you,
O there to have a wife, a wife, a wife,
    O tis a smart to my heart,
Tis a racke to my backe
    And to my belly.

3

All you that are Batchelers,
    Be learnd by crying Will,
When you are well to remaine so still,
    Better for to tarry,
And alone to lie,
    Than like a foole with a foole to crie:
A figge for such a wife, a wife, a wife,
    O what a life do I leade,
With a wife in my bed,
    I may not tell you,
O there to have a wife, a wife, a wife,
    O tis a smart to my heart,
Tis a racke to my backe
    And to my belly.

ANONYMOUS

*chil: I'll

IN SHERWOOD LIVDE STOUT ROBIN HOOD

ROBERT JONES

A MUSICALL DREAME
OR THE FOURTH BOOKE OF AYRES 1609

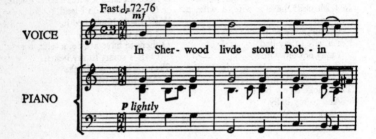

In Sher-wood livde stout Rob-in

Hood, An Arch-er great none great-er.

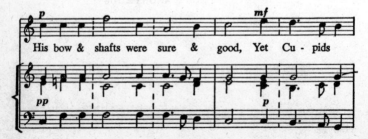

His bow & shafts were sure & good, Yet Cu-pids

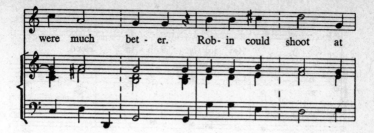

were much bet - er. Rob- in could shoot at

man - y a Hart and misse, Cu - pid at

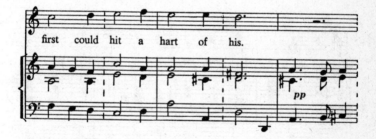

first could hit a hart of his.

Hey jol- ly Rob- in, Hoe jol- ly

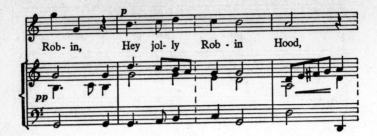

Rob- in,   Hey jol- ly   Rob - in   Hood,

Love finds out me   As   well   as   thee

To   fol - low me,   to   fol - low me,

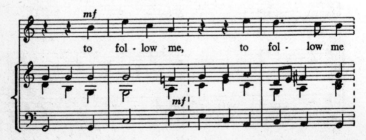

to   fol - low me,   to   fol - low me

to   the green   wood. _____

1

In Sherwood livde stout Robin Hood,
　　An Archer great none greater.
His bow & shafts were sure & good,
　　Yet Cupids were much beter.
Robin could shoot at many a Hart and misse,
　　Cupid at first could hit a hart of his.
　　　　　　Hey jolly Robin,
　　　　　　Hoe jolly Robin,
　　　　　Hey jolly Robin Hood,
　　　　　　Love finds out me
　　　　　　As well as thee
　　　　To follow me to the green wood.

2

A noble thiefe was Robin Hoode,
　　Wise was he could deceive him,
Yet Marrian in his bravest mood
　　Could of his heart bereave him,
No greater thiefe lies hidden under skies
　　Than beauty closely logde in womens eyes.
　　　　　　Hey jolly Robin. *etc.*

3

An Out-law was this Robin Hood,
　His life free and unruly,
Yet to faire Marrian bound he stood
　And loves debt payed her duely.
Whom curbe of stricktest law could not hold in,
　Love with obeydnes and a wink could winne.
　　　　　　Hey jolly Robin. *etc.*

4

Now end we home stout Robin Hood,
　Leave we the woods behind us,
Love passions must not be withstood,
　Love every where will find us.
I livde in field and towne, and so did he,
　I got me to the woods, love followed me.
　　　　　　Hey jolly Robin.

ANONYMOUS

194

ITE CALDI SOSPIRI

ROBERT JONES

A MUSICALL DREAME
OR THE FOURTH BOOKE OF AYRES 1609

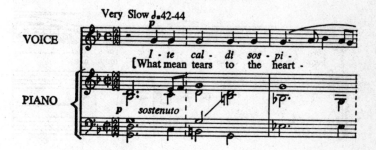

1) original: barline here
2) original: B♭

195

tà con - ten - - de E se
not en - dear _____ me. Though she

pre - go mor - ta - - le al ciel
hear not my weep - -ing, may heav -

_____ s'in - ten - de Mor - - te,
- en hear me: Grant me,

p cresc. poco a poco
_pp_ _cresc. poco a poco_

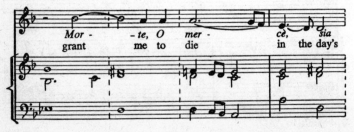

Mor - - te, O mer - ce, sia
grant me to die in the day's

1) original: D

197

mio   do - lo -   re.
wake   in sor -   row.

1) original: low G omitted

Ite caldi sospiri al freddo core,
Rompete il ghiaccio che pieta contende
E se prego mortale al ciel s'intende
Morte O merce sia fine al mio dolore.*

ANONYMOUS

ENGLISH METRICAL VERSION

What mean tears to the heartless? Then cease tomorrow:
Pity breeds no love where love could not endear me.
Though she hear not my weeping, may heaven hear me:
Grant me to die in the day's dying, not wake in sorrow.

C.S.K.

*(Go, warm sighs, to that cold heart and break the ice that resists all pity. If mortal prayer be heard in heaven, death, O to my thanks, may end my sorrow.)

THERE WAS A WYLY LADDE

THE MUSES GARDIN FOR DELIGHTS,
OR THE FIFT BOOKE OF AYRES 1610

ROBERT JONES

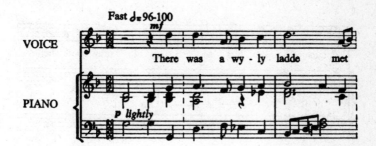

There was a wy - ly ladde met

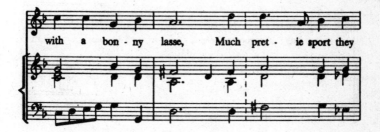

with a bon - ny lasse, Much pret - ie sport they

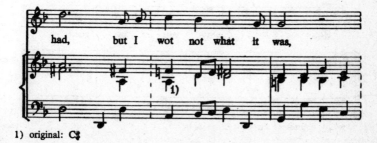

had, but I wot not what it was,

1) original: C♯

Hee woed her for a kisse, she

plaine - ly said him no, I pray quoth he,

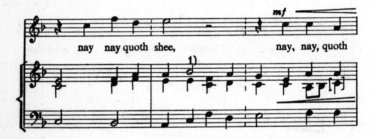

nay nay quoth shee, nay, nay, quoth

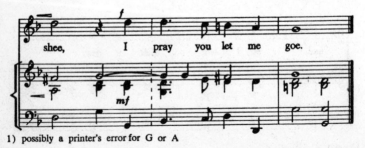

shee, I pray you let me goe.

1) possibly a printer's error for G or A

1

There was a wyly ladde met with a bonny lasse,
Much pretie sport they had, but I wot not what it was,
Hee woed† her for a kisse, she plainely said him no,
    I pray quoth he, nay nay quoth shee,
    I pray you let me goe.

2

Full many lovely tearms did passe in merrie glee,
He col'd* her in his armes and daunc't her on his knee,
And faine he would have paide such debts as he did owe,
    I pray quoth he, nay nay quoth shee,
    I pray you let me goe.

3

Sweete be you not so nice to gratifie a friend,
If kissing be a vice, my sute is at an end.
Noe noe it is the rule to learne a man to woe.
    I pray quoth he, nay nay quoth shee,
    I pray you let me goe.

4

For Cupid hath an eye to play a lovers part,
And swift his arrowes flie to leavell at the heart,
Thy beauty was my bane that brought me to his bowe,
    I pray quoth he, nay nay quoth shee,
    I pray you let me goe.

5

Good Sir alas you feede your fancie with conceit.
Sweete sweet how should we speede if lovers could not speake.
I speake but what I wish, the spirit wils me so,
    I pray quoth he, nay nay quoth shee,
    I pray you let me goe.

6

With that shee swore an Oath, and loth she was to breake it,
And so to please them both, he gave and shee did take it,
There was no labour lost, true amitie to show,
    Adew quoth he, nay, stay quoth shee,
    Let's kisse before you goe.

ANONYMOUS

†woed: wooed
*col'd: embraced

MISTERESSE MINE

THOMAS MORLEY   **THE FIRST BOOKE OF AYRES 1600**

Moderately slow ♩=63-66

VOICE

Miste - resse mine well may you fare,

PIANO

mf legato

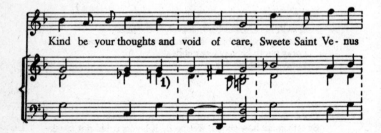

Kind be your thoughts and void of care, Sweete Saint Ve - nus

1)

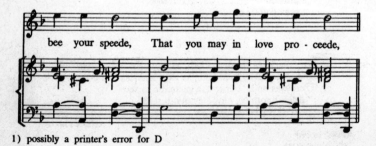

bee your speede, That you may in love pro - ceede,

1) possibly a printer's error for D

202

Coll mee and clip and kisse me too, So so so so so so true love should do.
do.

1) original: repeat written out in full

1

Misteresse mine well may you fare,
Kind be your thoughts and void of
   care,
Sweete Saint Venus bee your speede,
That you may in love proceede,
Coll* mee and clip and kisse me too,
So so so so so so true love should do.

2

This faire morning Sunnie bright,
That gives life to loves delight,
Everie hart with heate inflames,
And out cold affection blames.
Coll mee and clip and kisse me too,
So so so so so so true love should do.

3

In these woods are none but birds,
They can speake but silent words:
They are prettie harmelesse things,
They will shade us with their wings.
Coll mee and clip and kisse me too,
So so so so so so true love should do.

4

Never strive nor make no noyes,
Tis for foolish girles and boyes,
Everie childish thing can say,
Goe to, how now, pray away.
Coll mee and clip and kisse me too,
So so so so so so true love should do.

ANONYMOUS

*Coll: embrace

THOMAS MORLEY   **THE FIRST BOOKE OF AYRES 1600**

It was a lov - er and his lasse, With a

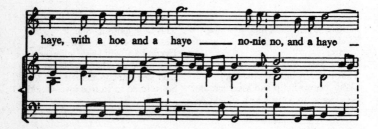

haye, with a hoe and a haye ___ no-nie no, and a haye ___

___ no - nie, no - nie no, That

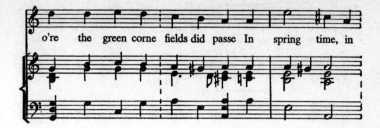

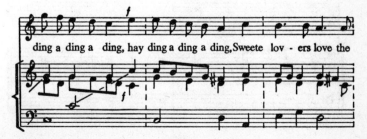

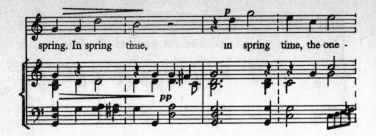

spring. In spring time, in spring time, the one -

ly pret - tie ring time, When Birds do sing, hay

ding a ding a ding, hay ding a ding a ding, hay

ding a ding a ding, Sweete lov - ers love the spring.

1

It was a lover and his lasse,
With a haye, with a hoe and a haye nonie no,
That o're the green corne fields did passe
In spring time, the onely prettie ring time,
When Birds do sing, hay ding a ding a ding,
Sweete lovers love the spring.

2

Betweene the Akers of the rie,
With a hay, with a ho and a hay nonie no,
These prettie Countrie fooles would lie,
In spring time, the onely prettie ring time,
When Birds doe sing, hay ding a ding a ding,
Sweete lovers love the spring.

3

This Carrell they began that houre,
With a hay, with a ho and a hay nonie no,
How that a life was but a flower,
In spring time, the onely prettie ring time,
When Birds doe sing, hay ding a ding a ding,
Sweete lovers love the spring.

4

Then prettie lovers take the time,
With a hay, with a ho and a hay nonie no,
For love is crowned with the prime,
In spring time, the onely prettie ring time,
When Birds doe sing, hay ding a ding a ding,
Sweete lovers love the spring.

WORDS BY WILLIAM SHAKESPEARE (?)

FAIRE IN A MORNE

THOMAS MORLEY   THE FIRST BOOKE OF AYRES 1600

Faire in a morne oh fair-est morne was

ev- er morne so faire, When as the sun but

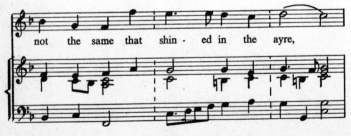

not the same that shin-ed in the ayre,

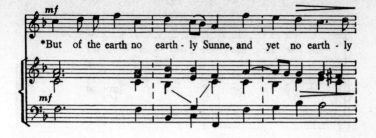

*But of the earth no earth-ly Sunne, and yet no earth-ly

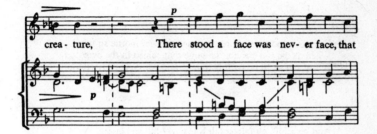

crea-ture, There stood a face was nev-er face, that

car-ried such a fea-ture.

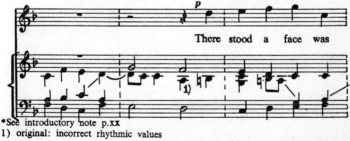

There stood a face was

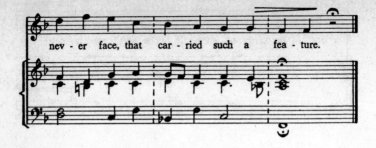

never face, that car-ried such a fea-ture.

1

Faire in a morne oh fairest morne was ever morne so faire,
When as the sun but not the same that shined in the ayre,
*But of the earth no earthly Sunne, and yet no earthly creature,
There stoode a face was never face, that carried such a feature.

2

And on a hill, oh fairest hill was never hill so blessed,
There stood a man was never man for no man so distressed,
This man had hap O happie man, no man so hapt as he,
For none had hap to see the hap, that he had hapt to see.

3

As he, behold, this man beheld, he saw so faire a face,
The which would daunt the fairest here, and staine the bravest grace,
Pittie he cried, and pittie came, and pittied for his paine,
That dying would not let him die, but gave him life againe.

4

For joy whereof he made such mirth, that all the world did ring,
And *Pan* for all his *Nimphs* came forth, to heare the shepherds sing,
But such a song song never was, nor nere will be againe,
Of *Philida* the shepheards Queene, and *Coridon* the swaine.

NICHOLAS BRETON

*See introductory note p.xx

NOW PEEP, BOE PEEP

THE FIRST BOOKE OF
SONGS OR AYRES 1605

FRANCIS PILKINGTON

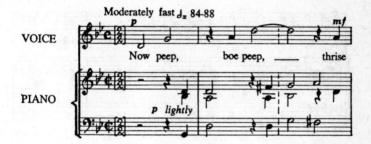

Moderately fast ♩= 84-88

VOICE

PIANO

Now peep, boe peep, ____ thrise

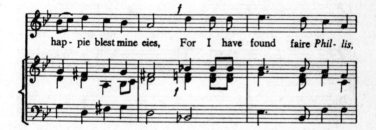

hap - pie blest mine eies, For I have found faire *Phil - lis,*

for I have found faire *Phil-lis* where she lies,

Up- on her bed, _____ with

armes un- spred, _ all fast a - sleepe, Un - maskt her

face, thrise hap - pie grace, fare - well, fare -

well my sheepe, Look ____ to your

212

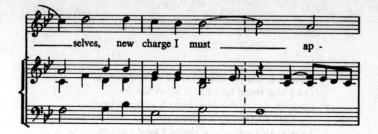

selves, new charge I must ————— ap -

prove, *Phil - lis* doth sleepe,

Phil - lis doth sleepe, and I must

guard ————— my Love. Love.

1

Now peep, boe pee, thrise happie blest mine eies,
For I have found faire *Phillis* where she lies,
Upon her bed, with armes unspred, all fast asleepe,
Unmaskt her face, thrise happie grace, farewell my sheepe.
Look to your selves, new charge I must approve,
Phillis doth sleepe, and I must guard my Love.

2

Now peep boe pee, mine eyes, to see your blisse,
Phillis closd eyes atrackts you, hers to kisse:
Oh may I now perform my vow, loves joy t'impart,
Assay the while how to be-guile, farewell faint hart.
Taken she is, new joyes I must approve,
Phillis doth sleep, and I will kisse my love.

3

Now peep, boe peep, be not too bould my hand,
Wake not thy *Phillis*, feare shee doe with-stand:
Shee stirs alas, alas, alas I faint in spright,
Shee opes her eie, unhappie I, farewell delight.
Awakt shee is, new woes I must approve,
Phillis awakes, and I must leave my Love.

ANONYMOUS

REST SWEET NIMPHS

FRANCIS PILKINGTON

THE FIRST BOOKE OF
SONGS OR AYRES 1605

Rest sweet Nimphs let gould - en

sleepe Charme your star bright - er eies,

Whiles my Lute the watch doth keep With pleas - ing sim - pa -

215

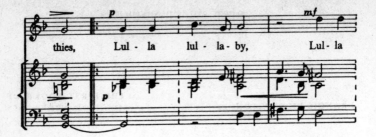

thies, Lul - la lul - la - by, Lul - la

lul - la - by, Sleepe sweet - ly, sleep sweet - ly,

let noth - ing af - fright ye, In

calme con - tent - ments lie. lie.

Rest sweet Nimphs let goulden sleepe
Charme your star brighter eies,
Whiles my Lute the watch doth keep
With pleasing simpathies,
Lulla lullaby, Lulla lullaby,
Sleepe sweetly, sleep sweetly, let nothing affright ye,
In calme contentments lie.

2

Dreame faire virgins of delight
And blest Elizian groves:
Whiles the wandring shades of night
Resemble your true loves:
Lulla lullaby, Lulla lullaby
Your kisses your blisses send them by your wishes,
Although they be not nigh.

Thus deare damzells I do give
Good night and so am gone:
With your hartes desires long live,
Still joy, and never mone.
Lulla lullaby, Lulla lullaby
Hath pleasd you and easd you, & sweet slumber sezd you,
And now to bed I hie.

ANONYMOUS

WHEN LAURA SMILES

PHILIP ROSSETER   A BOOKE OF AYRES 1601

When Lau-ra smiles her sight re-
The earth & heaven viewes with de-

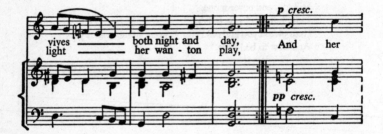

vives ——— both night and day,
light ——— her wan-ton play, And her

speech with ev - er ——— flow - ing mu - sicke

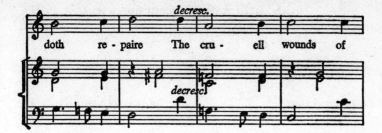

doth re-paire The cru-ell wounds of

sor-row and un-tam'd des-paire.

 1

When Laura smiles her sight revives
  both night and day,
The earth & heaven viewes with delight her wanton play,
And her speech with ever-flowing musicke doth repaire
The cruell wounds of sorrow and
  untam'd despaire.

2

The [daintie] sprites that [still] remaine in fleeting aire
Affect for pastime to untwine her
  tressed haire,
And the birds thinke sweete Aurora
  mornings Queene doth shine
From her bright sphere when Laura
  shewes her lookes devine.

3

Dianas eyes are not adorn'd with
  greater power
Than Lauras when she lists awhile for
  sport to loure,
But when she her eyes encloseth,
  blindnes doth appeare
The chiefest grace of beautie sweete-
  lie seated there.

4

Love hath no fire but what he steales
  from her bright eyes,
Time hath no power, but that which in
  her pleasure lyes,
For she with her devine beauties all
  the world subdues,
And fils with heav'nly spirits my humble muse.

THOMAS CAMPIAN

HEY HO, TO THE GREENWOOD[1]

Round for 3 voices

DAVID MELVILL

BOOK OF ROUNDELS 1612

Moderately Slow ♩=66-69

VOICE

Hey ho, to the green-wood now let us go, Sing hey and ho, And there shall we find both buck and doe, Sing hey and ho, The hart and hind and the lit-tle pret-ty roe, Sing hey and ho.

1) attributed to William Byrd
2) note values reduced by one-half

Hey ho, to the greenwood now let us go,
    Sing hey and ho,
And there shall we find both buck and doe,
    Sing hey and ho,
The hart and hind and the little pretty roe,
    Sing hey and ho.

ANONYMOUS

JOLLY SHEPHERD

Round for 3 voices

DAVID MELVILL

BOOK OF ROUNDELS 1612

VOICE

Jolly shepherd and upon a hill as he sat, So loud he blew his little horn and kept right well his gait, Early in a morning late in an evening And ever blew this little boy so merrily piping, Terliter lo, terliter lo, terliter lo terli! Terliter lo, terliter lo, terliter lo terli!

Jolly shepherd and up on a hill as he sat,
So loud he blew his little horn and kept right well his gait,
Early in a morning late in an evening
And ever blew this little boy so merrily piping,
Terliter lo, terliter lo, terliter lo terli!
Terliter lo, terliter lo, terliter lo terli!

ANONYMOUS

221

NOW GOD BE WITH OLD SIMEON

Round for 3 voices

DAVID MELVILL   BOOK OF ROUNDELS 1612

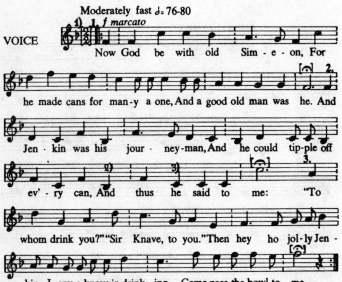

1) note values reduced by one-half
2) original: C
3) original: B♭

Now God be with old Simeon,
For he made cans for many a one,
And a good old man was he.
And Jenkin was his journeyman,
And he could tipple off ev'ry can,
And thus he said to me:
   "To whom drink you?"
   "Sir Knave, to you."
Then hey ho jolly Jenkin,
I spy a knave in drinking,
Come pass the bowl to me.

ANONYMOUS

222

MUSING

Round for 4 voices

DAVID MELVILL

BOOK OF ROUNDELS 1612

1) note values reduced by one-half

Musing my own self all alone,
I heard a maid making great moan,
With sobs and sighs and many a grievous moan
For that her maidenhead was gone.

ANONYMOUS

TO PORTSMOUTH

Round for 4 voices

DAVID MELVILL

BOOK OF ROUNDELS 1612

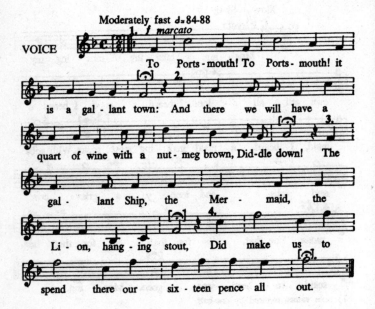

To Portsmouth! To Portsmouth! it is a gallant town:
And there we will have a quart of wine with a nutmeg brown,
Diddle down!
The gallant Ship, the Mermaid, the Lion, hanging stout,
Did make us to spend there our sixteen pence all out.
Diddle down!

ANONYMOUS

SING WE NOW MERRILY

Round for 10 voices[1]

DAVID MELVILL   BOOK OF ROUNDELS 1612

1) Melvill also suggests 11 voices, in which case 2 measures of rest must be
added before returning to "sing we merrily."

> Sing we now merrily,
> Our purses be empty,
> Hey ho!
> Let him take care
> That lists to spare
> For I will not do so;
> Who can sing so merry a note
> As he that cannot change a groat!
> Hey ho,
> Trollie lollie, trollie lollie lo!

ANONYMOUS

225

O LUSTY MAY

Part song for 4 voices

DAVID MELVILL

BOOK OF ROUNDELS 1612

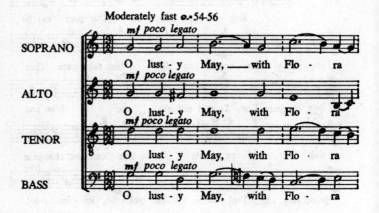

sheen Pre - lu - cent beams be - fore the

sheen Pre - lu - cent beams be - fore the

sheen Pre - lu - cent beams be - fore the

sheen Pre - lu - cent beams be - fore the

day, the day, By the Di -

day, the day, By the

day, the day, By the Di -

day, the day, By the

an - a grow - eth

Di - an - a grow - eth, grow - eth

an - a grow - eth, grow - eth

Di - an - a grow - eth

1) original: F♮

227

green Through glad - ness of this
green Through glad - ness of this
green Through glad - ness of this
green Through glad - ness of this

lust - -y May, this
lust - -y May, this lust -
lust - -y May, this
lust - -y May, of this

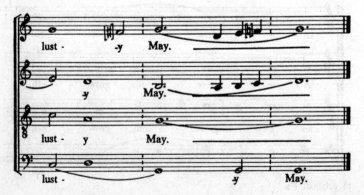

lust - -y May.
y May.
lust - y May.
lust - y May.

1

O lusty May, with Flora Queen,
The balmë drops from Pheobus' sheen
Prelucent beams before the day,
By the Diana groweth green
Through gladness of this lusty May.

2

Then Hesperus that is so bright,
To woeful hearts he casteth light
Right pleasantly before the day,
And shows and sheds forth of that sight
Through gladness of this lusty May.

3

The birds on boughs of ev'ry sorth*
Send forth their notes and make great mirth
On banks that bloom on ev'ry brae,
And fare and fly o'er field and firth
Through gladness of this lusty May.

4

All lovers' hearts that are in care,
To their ladies they do repair
On fresh mornings before the day,
And are in mirth aye more and more
Through gladness of this lusty May.

5

Of all the monthës of the year,
To mirthful May there is no peer,
Then glist'ring garments are so gay,
Ye lovers all make merry cheer
Through gladness of this lusty May.

ANONYMOUS

*sorth: sort

229

DOE YOU NOT KNOW

Canzonet for 3 voices

THOMAS MORLEY

CANZONETS OR LITTLE SHORT SONGS
TO THREE VOYCES 1593

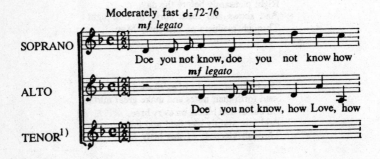

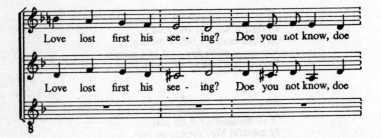

1) or Baritone

231

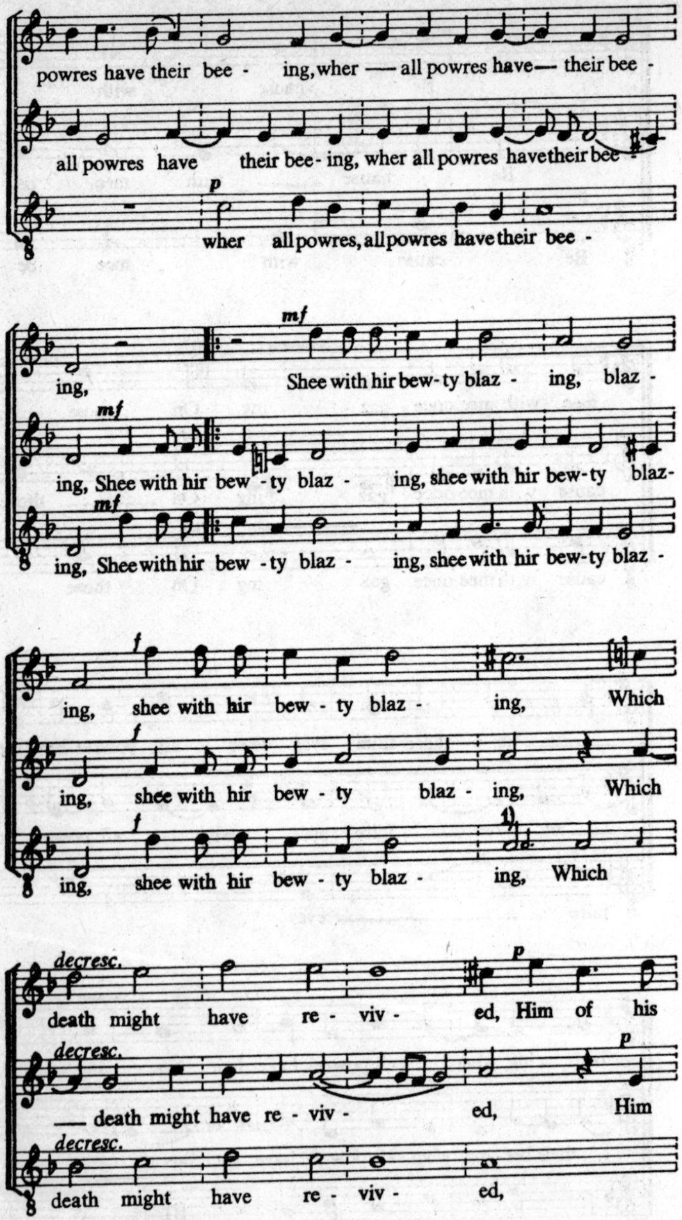

1) original: small notes on repeat

sight and mee of hart de - priv - ed, him of his sight and

of his sight and mee of hart de -priv - ed. him of his

Him of his sight and mee of

mee of hart de - priv - ed, - ed.

sight and mee of hart de-priv - ed. Shee with hir - ed.

hart de - priv - ed. Shee with hir - ed.

1) original: repeat written out in full

Doe you not know how Love lost first his seeing?
        Because with mee once gazing
On those faire eyes wher all powres have their beeing,
        Shee with hir bewty blazing,
        Which death might have revived,
Him of his sight and mee of hart deprived.

ANONYMOUS

233

ADEW SWEET AMARILLIS

Madrigal for 4 voices

THE FIRST SET OF
ENGLISH MADRIGALS 1598

JOHN WILBYE

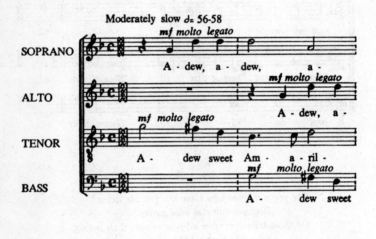

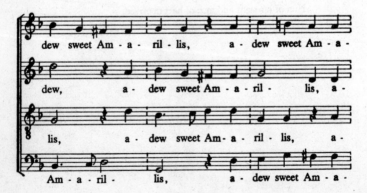

Somewhat faster

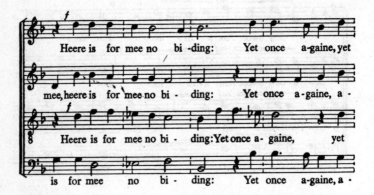

O —— heav - y tyd - ing,

O heav - y tyd - ing, Heere is for

O heav - y tyd - ing,

O heav - y tyd - ing, Heere

Heere is for mee no bi -ding: Yet once a-gaine, yet

mee, heere is for mee no bi - ding: Yet once a-gaine, a-

Heere is for mee no bi - ding: Yet once a- gaine, yet

is for mee no bi - ding: Yet once a-gaine, a -

once a-gaine, a - gaine, ere that I part —— with

gaine, ere that I part with

once a-gaine, a - gaine, ere that —— I part with

gaine, ere that I part with

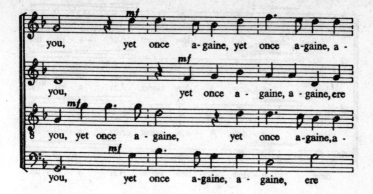

you, yet once a-gaine, yet once a-gaine, a-

you, yet once a - gaine, a - gaine, ere

you, yet once a-gaine, yet once a-gaine, a-

you, yet once a - gaine, a - gaine, ere

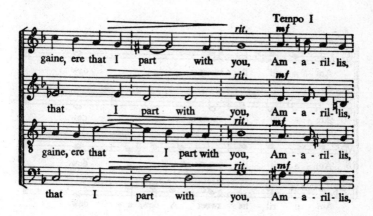

Tempo I

rit.

gaine, ere that I part with you, Am - a - ril - lis,

that I part with you, Am - a - ril - lis,

gaine, ere that I part with you, Am - a - ril - lis,

that I part with you, Am - a - ril - lis,

Am - a - ril - lis, sweet a - dew, a - dew,

Am - a - ril - lis, sweet a - dew, a -

Am - a - ril - lis, sweet a - dew, a - dew, a -

Am - a - ril - lis, sweet a - dew, a - dew, a -

Adew sweet Amarillis

For since to part your will is,

Adew sweet Amarillis:

    O heavy tyding,

   Heere is for mee no biding:

Yet once againe, ere that I part with you,

   Adew sweet Amarillis,

   Amarillis, sweet adew.

ANONYMOUS

INDEX OF FIRST LINES

INDEX OF POETS